About the Author

Susanna lives in the Northern Suburbs of Wollongong, south of Sydney, Australia where she works as a specialist teacher of students with learning difficulties. She also writes professionally as an author of educational resources in literacy areas for teachers. Her programs sell world-wide. Susanna has a passion for teaching, which combined with her love of writing affords her a busy, but highly rewarding lifestyle. Living so close to the south coast beaches on the east coast of Australia, Susanna's inspiration for her writing comes from the beautiful coastal and mountainous environments on her home doorstep.

Looking Back Without Anger

Susanna Elliot-Newth

Looking Back Without Anger

Olympia Publishers
London

www.olympiapublishers.com
OLYMPIA PAPERBACK EDITION

Copyright © Susanna Elliot-Newth 2024

The right of Susanna Elliot-Newth to be identified as author of this work has been asserted in accordance with sections 77 and 78 of the Copyright, Designs and Patents Act 1988.

All Rights Reserved

No reproduction, copy or transmission of this publication may be made without written permission.
No paragraph of this publication may be reproduced, copied or transmitted save with the written permission of the publisher, or in accordance with the provisions of the Copyright Act 1956 (as amended).

Any person who commits any unauthorised act in relation to this publication may be liable to criminal prosecution and civil claims for damage.

A CIP catalogue record for this title is available from the British Library.

ISBN: 978-1-80439-593-6

This book is memoir. It reflects the author's present recollections of experiences over time. Some names and characteristics have been changed, some events have been compressed, and some dialogue has been recreated.

First Published in 2024

Olympia Publishers
Tallis House
2 Tallis Street
London
EC4Y 0AB

Printed in Great Britain

Dedication

This book is dedicated to my friend Rosemary. I have never met anyone who has shown me such a caring response after reading any one of these stories. Such is a true friend.

Acknowledgements

I should like to thank my circle of readers who avidly read my weekly blogs, stories, sagas and poems. Without an audience, there is little point in writing. All of you have inspired me in different ways to tell this - my personal account of a very difficult time in my life. Thank you

Cover Design – Joshua Brown

'Great suffering is always a great teacher'
The Song of Roland
(11th Century French)

If suffering is such a great teacher,
then I welcome more experiences to grow in spirit.
When we experience true suffering,
we experience a greater sense of self.
If my suffering has helped others,
then it has achieved its purpose.
Releasing tears releases pain,
allowing hearts to love again.

A Feast of Rosemary

I look out upon a sea of colour
When spring is sprung her best,
Leaving poor winter desolate,
Gnarled and spectre grey.
Red cedar's colour now returning,
As his reddish tinged sweater
Adorns his gracious form.
The garden's blossoms - such vivid colours
Are a feast to my eyes,
Each fragrant petal enticing
Their pollinators.
White cedar's white and lilac flowers
Sing gracefully in the breeze.
Such show-offs here are born.
I turn my attention now to the herbs,
These delicious, sweet meats -
Such treats that blend so gracefully
As perfect garnish.
Rosemary, my favourite of all,
Stands tall, her arms outstretched –
Gives me the warmest hug.

Preface

There are some stories that must be told, not for entertainment purposes and not for educational interest but because their content and their context is beyond reasonable comprehension. Many people experience abusive situations: the school bully, workplace harassment, an unexpected physical or sexual assault, or the unwanted inappropriate attentions of a parent for that person's gratification. None of these situations can ever be excused because they change the way the victims live their lives.

In 2011, I published a little book called, *Tears on the Inside*.

Tears on the outside fall to the ground
And are gently washed away.
Tears on the inside fall on the soul
And stay... and stay... and stay...

I received many feedback notations from readers, many of whom stated the stories were a 'little stretched' or 'implausible' because the situations were too difficult to imagine really happening. Sadly, those readers were wrong – they did happen. If anything, the recounts in this book were played down, so as not to provide too bleak or traumatic read for audiences.

I have a story to tell. 'Looking Back Without Anger' presents encounters I experienced from the age of two to eighteen years of age. To understand why these situations happened, one must understand that in the 1950s, very little was recognised about many mental health issues that people presented with. There were no child protection agencies that people could report child abuse incidents to; there were no medical practitioners who would have diagnosed my mother's mental health condition in such a way that a treatment program could have been available for her; and there were no persons out there in my world who would have dared to challenge my mother in any way. So, no-one came to the aid of a very small child.

I never met my maternal grandmother. She had been incarcerated in a mental institution for the mentally insane long before I was born, and my mother never spoke of her. I only met my mother's father briefly, just before he died. So, I have no knowledge of any historical event that caused my mother's mental state or condition. Her two sisters never appeared to exhibit the bizarre behaviours my mother fell foul to, and on the very brief occasions I did meet with them, I never divulged secrets from my illusive world. (I don't think they would have believed me!)

These stories are as they happened, and I make no apologies and I have nothing to be ashamed of. I did nothing wrong!

Prologue

There is nothing more nurturing, or so natural, than hearing children call out the word, 'Mum.' This universal and commonly used word falls off every child's lips without them ever giving a thought to the place this very special lady is placed in their lives.

The same can be said for the word, 'Dad,' except that the use of this endearment does not carry with it a deeper, immeasurable measure of love and family unity that the female counterpart does.

'Mum,' or its equivalent across all languages and cultures derives from the first sounds a baby makes as it begins to develop language.

So, why is it that this word is alien in Susanna's own lexicon of words? The word, 'Dad' too, is similarly absent. As a young child growing up, she was never permitted to use either of these two terms. She remembers quite clearly, at the age of three, being told to use 'other' words that her parents had devised.

As Susanna grew and interacted with friends from her school, she would be asked why she referred to her parents using these other words. Susanna's response was always, "I'm not allowed to refer to my parents as 'Mum' and 'Dad'.

Later in life Susanna would look back and recall that this was a significant factor in how she thinks her mother, more than her father, viewed her relationship with her daughter.

She recalls that her mother never stated that she was 'proud' of her daughter, despite the many successes Susanna achieved during the time she was at school. When she was in Year 6, she was asked to teach a Year 3 class English for an hour a week. In Year 8 she was placed on a timetable of teaching Year 7 English and Year 8 French, and then again in Year 11 she was given a full-time teaching load of English and French. No other student in either of these schools was ever selected to 'teach' other students.

From Years 8-12 Susanna won the school's prestigious Public Speaking Award. When she foolishly allowed her mother to discover this prize, when she was in Year 9, her mother had scoffed at her, "You stupid child, they only gave you that because they felt sorry for you!"

At the age of sixteen, Susanna was selected by the local council to do the Outward-Bound Leadership Course, held in Wales. At the end of the course, she was selected to be part of a small group of adventurers to climb the Himalayas – an honour of the highest standing, as she was the youngest participant ever to undergo the Outward-Bound challenge, let alone be considered for this elite expedition.

After successfully trekking in the snow and ice conditions of Nepal, Susanna used this experience to qualify for the Duke of Edinburgh Gold Award Scheme expedition section. She was invited to receive this award from Prince Phillip, a ceremony she attended with her father. Two years later, Susanna's sister too received this same Duke of Edinburgh Award. When a group of relatives once commented to her how wonderful her sister's achievement was, and enquired why she had never done this course, Susanna had simply looked at them and said, "I did, two years ago!"

They had been stunned.

"But your mother never said anything to us!"

"No, of course not!"

Throughout Susanna's entire childhood, her mother had never said a kind word to her. There was never a smile, or friendly hug, or even a pat on the back – there was only criticism and castigation. When asked once if she were ever naughty as a child, Susanna had replied, "How could I be? If she treated me like this when I was good, what the f _ _ _ would she have done to me if she had, had - justification?" No, Susanna learned early on in her life, that if she were to survive, then she had to be beyond reproach.

In closing, I bear my mother no malice. I accepted that she must have experienced significant trauma in her childhood and for which she had never received any treatment. I thank her too, for the opportunities she gave me to learn and grow in spirit. I look back without anger and embrace these difficult times because they are gifts - gifts that help me be who I am today.

A feature of all the books I have written is the inclusion of poetry to convey messages. Poetic verse can craft more succinctly what prose finds clumsy.

Throughout Their Lives

When babies and very young children look
At me, they see butterflies in my hair.
As they grow, their link to the spirit realm
Fades and their focus then, becomes my heart
That beats a rhyme and rhythm connection,
Reminding them that spirit protects them
Throughout their lives.
When children connect to me in lessons,
They feel that strong pulsating energy.
My spiritual link to the Heavens
Awakens their own knowledge of this realm
That they left not too long ago, when born.
It reassures them that God protects them
Throughout their lives.
God sent Jesus Christ to teach us lessons –
Lessons we must learn - to grow in spirit.
There is no other purpose in our lives.
There can be no greater purpose than that!
I connect to children of all ages,
And will always maintain this connection
Throughout their lives.
This fate gifted me from the Heavens
Exceeds any other needs I might have.
Spending the time, I do, with my students
Is precious time that makes them feel special.

We bond in ways their parents cannot know,
Or understand, but know they benefit –
Throughout their lives.

A Babe in Arms

The earliest memory I have is standing in the little scullery kitchen of my parent's Harrow house looking into the crib of a baby. My younger sister had been born a few weeks earlier and had just been fed. As she is exactly two years, two months and two days younger than me, the date is the end of January 1953. I am two years three months old.

I am expected to wash the nappy that has just been changed and hang it on the washing line. Obediently, I take the soiled items to the outside lavatory to deposit the excrement, flush the toilet and then use the carbolic soap in the outside sink to scrub the cloths clean.

I remember my little fingers being sore from so much scrubbing, and I had difficulty wringing the cloths dry enough to hang on the line. To even reach the sink I had to use a chair to stand on - one that wobbled and made me feel anything but safe. But do the job, I do – to do a bad job would result in my mother punching me in the head, something she did frequently.

The kitchen had a washing line pulley that could be lowered to hang washing on and then be hauled up high to let the items dry. This scullery area was always warm, as my mother used a coal furnace that heated this room and the water. Going outside to the lavatory and outhouse sink was below freezing point in January, and I remember that snow lay on the ground in mounds of ice.

Having squeezed as much water from the cloths as I could, I

return to the kitchen and begin unwinding the pulley. It is hard work. Again, I have to stand on a chair to reach the notch, and then carefully step down as the pulley lowers. It is easier to lower than it is to haul up, especially when other wet clothing items are added. But do the job, I do – no complaints, no whinges and no help from my mother, and certainly no thanks.

No, saying 'thank you' to this daughter of hers was not in her vocabulary, and yet Susanna was the most competent little two-year-old anyone would ever meet. My name is not Susanna, by the way - I was christened Susan Mary, but changed my name later in life because the way my mother said my name was too cruel a memory for me.

I did not know at this time that my mother had a mental health disorder. Later I learned that the famous actress, Joan Crawford, also exhibited similar personality traits to my mother, and that both ladies' obsessive compulsive and personality disorders went undiagnosed. This gave them a licence to treat their children as they saw fit, with no accountability for any abuse they imposed on them.

My mother was never a happy lady. She and my father had met at the end of the war, when they were both stationed in India. My father had been a captain in the army and needed hospital treatment before returning home to England. My mother had been his nurse. He fell in love with her. In 1946 she was a very attractive and gregarious young girl – one who certainly caught his eye. My mother had not fallen in love with him, though. Her background was a working class, Lancashire lass, and my father was a middle to upper class Londoner. My mother saw an opportunity to better herself, and so they married before returning home to England.

The first house they purchased was a lovely bungalow in

Northwood, a middle-class suburb in North London. When their third daughter was conceived, they moved to the larger four-story house in downtown Harrow. This house was over one hundred years old and not a welcoming, comfortable house for a family to live in, but it had four bedrooms and two sitting rooms.

On returning to England in 1946, my parents had realised immediately that their marriage was not likely to be a success. In moving to the Harrow house, they both established separate lives, allocating themselves the two sitting rooms. Any communal family time was spent in the scullery room, which from recollection was not often.

In 1953 my father was studying to be an accountant, and at the same time working for British Rail in London. He would leave early in the morning and return home late at night. On entering the house, he would eat a plate of steamed food left for him by his wife and then hide himself away in his sitting room. There was no sharing of any conversation. At the weekends, he would leave early each morning and study at the local library until late. In the summertime, he enjoyed going to the cricket.

My mother was happier with him out of the house. She worked as a district nurse from eight a.m. until one thirty p.m. and then as a hospital sister at the local Harrow Hospital from eleven p.m. until seven a.m. At the weekends she worked in the mornings and would be 'on call' in the afternoons and evenings.

So, who looked after her children? Really good question!

Living in Fear

I never knew just what was wrong,
But sensed it wasn't what I'd done.
I tried to find so many ways
To help me through each troubled day.
My mother's illness at that time,
Undiagnosed and undefined.
She couldn't help the things she did,
That caused me grief I couldn't rid.
As each day dawned my fear and dread
Would send such terror through my head.
Surviving day alone at night,
I'd cry for hours till dawn's first light.
Now that I'm grown and life's moved on
I can't forgive the harm so done.
But now instead I try to see
These hardships set my spirit free.
I really value what life brings
With each new day my heart now sings.

Looking back on my life I have come to realise that these experiences have given me extraordinary insight into people's personal and social behaviours and the empathy to offer counsel of some efficacy to others suffering similar experiences.

I have also come to realise the **reality** of the spiritual world and have developed an avid interest in seeking knowledge about the afterlife.

Murder on Her Mind

In 1953, after giving birth to her third daughter, my mother returned to her work as a district nurse. One of her patients looked after the baby, who was taken to her house each morning and collected at the end of her day shift.

No-one looked after me, and my older sister attended school. My mother's routine was to care for her patients until lunchtime and then go to bed with her baby in the afternoons, feeding her as needed, until she went out to work at night.

She never did any housework, except to cook herself lunch and leave her husband's food on a plate to steam later that night. No thought at all was given to me. Alone in the house all day I became fiercely independent, able to care and entertain myself. I had no toys – I didn't need toys – I was always given chores to do. One of these was to clean the silver.

The box of silver cutlery had been a wedding gift from friends in India, and the other assortments of jugs, tea sets and vases had been given to her from her mother. None of these items were ever used, but of course had to be religiously cleaned, polished and replaced in their allotted showcases each week. (I knew that this chore had been a ploy to keep me busy). On the one occasion I had not cleaned these items, she had taken to me with a large stick, and had banished me upstairs for the remainder of the day. Of course, the next day I had diligently completed the task as I did every week after that.

Other jobs she set out for me to do were vacuuming the stairs

– only ever the stairs, dusting the furniture, washing clothes, cleaning the indoor and outdoor tiles and wiping down the windows that used to get condensation drips. I never minded any of these jobs, as they kept me busy. I also took pride in my work. Even to this day I am extremely fastidious about how I keep my house. I was always hungry, though.

In England at this time, people did not have the variety of machines and appliances we have today. There was no refrigerator. Food was stored in a pantry that was made of stone. This kept food cold. It was never a problem in the winter, as food did not require to be cooled, but in the summer months penicillin mould grew on all food items in this pantry. If I wanted something to eat, I would go into this pantry and collect a slice of bread (that always had mould around the crust), marmite (that never went mouldy because of the salt content) and dripping (pig fat). I smile to this day when I think how I used to use my fingers to pull off the crusts, smear the dripping over the bread and blob a dollop of marmite in the centre. (Delicious – absolutely not!)

In my current life, I recently had a guest who stayed a few nights a week in my house. At dinner, she would always say, "Susanna, this is delicious!"

Nothing I ever ate as a child was delicious – this is not a word I ever use to describe food! Sitting in that cold pantry, eating bread and dripping, was anything but delicious. Often there was no marmite to override the taste of the fat, as the jar was too tight to twist open. There was one occasion when I used a knife to lever the lid off and sliced my thumb badly. Blood had gushed out all over the food sitting in pots, that I was not allowed to eat. My mother had been furious at having to throw this food away and had smacked me harshly.

The day my father was sick, was the day things changed.

It had been a Monday morning. His wife had not returned from her night shift yet, and he had not given a thought to the three small children living in the house. Why should he? He had always just got himself washed and dressed, eaten his breakfast and left by seven a.m. This man had become accustomed to leaving the house as early as he could and returning as late as he could. He was afforded the luxury of cereal and milk for breakfast and a steamed dinner at night. This man had no awareness of how his children were being cared for – or not – until now!

Still upstairs in bed, when his wife returned home, she did not communicate with him but just collected the baby and set off immediately for her day shift. My older sister had left for school, and I was downstairs cleaning the kitchen. He had come downstairs looking for breakfast.

"Susie, what are you doing?" the man had stared open-mouthed at his little two and a half-year-old daughter. (I don't know what he thought I did, or where I went during the day, but what he saw that morning he could not believe!)

My language at this age was not well progressed. Having spent all my time in the house, with little contact with the outside world, two parents who never spoke to me in conversational tones and two sisters who for varying reasons did not speak to me, it was not surprising I was not talking at this time. My father had quietly picked up the bucket and cloths, disposed of the water and carried me upstairs to spend the morning with him. My mother had been furious when she had returned home - furious because she had been caught out and furious because her usual afternoon nap had been thwarted. That night she and her husband had rowed viciously. This was the first time I went to bed and pressed my ears tight shut, so that I could hear no sounds, a practice I then continued every night until I left when I was eighteen.

The next week my grandmother arrived. There are no words to convey my mother's response. From the onset she had hated the lady. To me, she seemed sweet and kind, and she got on well with my father. The weather in England in May was beginning to become warmer, and we would go for walks during the day. At anytime my grandmother was inside the house when my mother was home, the poor lady was subjected to a tirade of verbal abuse. At my young age, these arguments to me were frightening – not because I could understand the language used (I couldn't) but because they were so intensely angry.

It was about a month later when things started happening. My grandmother started to complain of feeling unwell. As my mother was a nurse, no-one in our house was ever permitted to see a doctor, and so my grandmother took to her room. Being totally dependent on my mother now for her daily needs, my mother kept her bedridden.

(She had planned it! She had been so irate this lady had moved in, that the only way she could live with her was to keep her medicated and in bed all day). My father never asked any questions – he just accepted what his wife said.

I turned three in October of that year and had begun to talk. I think it was my grandmother who brought my speech along. As soon as she began talking to me, I was able to chat to her. I still remember those times. My chats with my grandmother, though were short-lived. Once she had been confined to her bed, she was kept asleep all day and all night. Within the space of three months, these three incidents happened.

Fire Fire

I woke up. It was dark and the house was very quiet. I could smell smoke, and so got out of bed to investigate. My bedroom was immediately next door to my grandmother's room, and as I stepped out onto the landing, I could see clouds of smoke coming through the bottom of the door. The smell of smoke out here was very strong. Without thinking, I burst into my grandmother's room, saw that her bed was on fire, immediately pulled the electric blanket plug out of the wall socket, ripped the blanket and all her bedding off her bed and rolled it up in a giant ball to douse the flames. Smoke billowed into my face, and I could scarcely breathe. I remember, it was also extremely hot and burned my hands.

Looking across at my grandmother's frail figure lying in bed, what confused me was how she could sleep so soundly through such an incident. Looking back to the mounds of burning blankets, what confused me again was why, or how, the blankets were so wet. At the time I did not ask questions – I was too young. Years later, however, I knew that my mother had orchestrated the incident. She had deliberately and cruelly poisoned my grandmother to make her ill, given her sleeping tablets to keep her asleep all day and night and then doused her electric blanket with water to make it catch fire. In those days, electric blankets went on top of the bed, not underneath.

(Yes, she had intended to kill the lady.)

Flaming Fury

The next incident occurred about a month later. Being

November, the evenings were getting very chilly now. Our house had no heating systems except the boiler in the kitchen that heated the house water. There was never any heating upstairs. On entering this realm of the house, I could always see my breath in the autumn and winter months. This night I awoke to the smell of heat. I could feel the heat emanating through the adjoining wall of the room next door – my bed felt hot!

Even being so young, my instincts knew something was savagely wrong and I feared the worst. Getting quickly out of bed and stepping onto the landing, I could see that lights were on downstairs. My parents had retreated to their own rooms and were oblivious to the situation developing upstairs. Looking across to my grandmother's room, I could see and feel a wall of heat coming through the bottom of the door. All I remember seeing was red. As I cautiously opened the door, the heat hit me. I could scarcely breathe. In the middle of the room was a kerosene heater with flames extending at least a foot into the air. The room was intensely hot.

As I looked across at my grandmother, I wondered how she could sleep through all this heat. She didn't stir – she was out cold! (This juxta positional moment is one I will never forget!)

I didn't think – I just acted. Using the little finger of my left hand, I pulled the kerosene heater out of the room onto the landing. It was a tripod model, made of metal, and intensely hot. I wasn't concerned for myself – only for my grandmother. Once on the landing, I turned the wick down. I was horrified – at three years of age I knew this wasn't right! I became agitated as I turned the wick down, as it took so long for the flames to die down and finally extinguish themselves. I then quietly went downstairs to inform my father of what I'd done.

Sitting together upstairs looking at the heater, he had asked me, "Susie, are you hurt?"

I had shown him my burnt finger, and he had just looked at me. No more was ever said of the incident.

(Yes, my mother had intended to kill the lady!)

The Weekend Escape

It was just after New Year, and my father had a week off work. He made plans to go to Europe for the week, leaving on the Friday and returning the following Thursday. My mother never agreed to go away anywhere, not even out for the day, always using her nursing job as her excuse. "John, I can't possibly go anywhere – I'm on call!"

However, on this occasion she did!

My father worked for British Rail and so we were all afforded free first-class travel anywhere in England and neighbouring European countries. He chose to take us to Belgium. It was wonderful! I loved the train to Dover but not so much the boat across to Ostend because the sea was very rough. Sitting in the final train to Brussels was exciting. I wondered what our hotel would be like. My father was so excited too. He had arranged for someone to keep an eye on his mother, and so had sat back to enjoy a week with his family.

Dinner in the hotel was memorable – we never had dinner at home! My mother had fussed about the cost but had eaten her meal none the less. The next morning at breakfast is when it had all happened. A telegram was delivered by the concierge to my father. People did not use telephones for overseas conversations at this time, and it was common for official notices to be transmitted in this telegram format. A telegram usually meant bad news!

I remember sitting next to my mother on her left. She had appeared fidgety when the saucer with the correspondence had been handed to my father.

"Dear, something terrible has happened?" he had looked at his wife.

She had then taken the letter and read the contents. It was from the Harrow police, who had been called to the house on the Friday night. The ceiling in my grandmother's room had collapsed, falling directly onto my grandmother.

The neighbour looking after the lady in our absence had gone in to give my grandmother her dinner and had been shocked to find her buried in rubble.

An ambulance had been called to take her to hospital.

The poor lady recovered but never returned to our house. My father arranged for her to live out her remaining years with his sister in Canada.

Did the hospital do any enquiry into my grandmother's medical condition? She had been bedridden for over two months, never once getting out of bed.

Did the police do any enquiry into why the ceiling had collapsed, other than to state they had found the debris saturated in water?

No…

On reading the letter, my mother had immediately stated she was returning to London and that my father was to stay with us for the planned week's holiday. (So, that had been her ploy!)

"No, dear, you stay with the children. She is my mother. I'll go."

(Gosh, he did not know his wife! There was no way she was going to stay with us on holiday!)

Sitting next to my mother that morning, I could feel her anxiety. I can read body language as if I'm reading a book. I can also read people's energy, even when not in their company. I wondered, "What kind of a person was my mother?"

Had she had murder on her mind?

Her weekend escape had certainly helped her escape any enquiry, and I know without a shadow of doubt that she orchestrated her alibi. She knew the police would never prove she had deliberately crept up to the ceiling and doused it with water five days in a row prior to leaving for Brussels. How do I know this? Because I saw her fetch the ladder and climb up into the attic. I watched her for five consecutive days, and I knew what she was doing.

(She also knew that I was watching her!)

Looking across the breakfast table at my mother, who was now staring worriedly at the telegram, all she said was, "Then we'd all better pack and go home."

The incident was never mentioned again.

(Yes, my mother had intended to kill the lady, and I had thwarted all her plans. No wonder she then hated me for the rest of my childhood, and no wonder I then became her target for taunts, many of which are too embarrassing and too cruel to detail in these next stories. Only the ones I can live with are included).

I'm going to include this poem here. It is found on a tombstone in the cemetery of Coventry Cathedral (UK). Sometimes we must accept that bad things happen, and in knowing that choose the right action to take, and not to make the same mistakes ourselves.

Good Digestion

Give me a good digestion Lord,
And give me something to digest.
Give me a healthy body Lord,
With sense to keep it at its best.
Give me a healthy mind Oh Lord,
To keep the good and pure in sight,
That seeing sin in not appalled,
But finds a way to set it right.
Give me a sense of humour Lord.
Give me the grace to see a joke -
To get some happiness out of life
And pass it on to other folk.

Anon

In this life I know I set myself some very difficult obstacles to surmount. I also know that I was meant to meet and marry my husband, Michael. He was my soul mate, and over the years he supported me unconditionally. In 2016 he was diagnosed with a brain tumour, and in 2018 he left. This poem is written as thanks to him.

To Michael,

Hard Challenges

I know that I've been given hard challenges to bear.
My life has not been easy, but I knew that you were there.
You helped me through the roughest times –
Your gentle love you shared,
Which helped to keep me going – a quality so rare.
I know that I've been given decisions hard to make,
But you were always with me to ease the hardest ache.
Your gentle love surrounded me
Each day I lay awake.
You helped to keep me going on this journey that I take.
I know that I've been given hard promises to keep,
Such burdens lying heavy upon my soul – I weep.
But you are always with me –
You share my secrets deep.
We'll take life's winding pathway until eternal sleep.
I know that I've been given hard challenges to fight,

To make the right decisions at close of day each night.
I've always kept my promise –
And always done what's right,
Now as your strength consumes me, I move towards the light.

Men From Mars

So, nothing changes then! With my grandmother now gone and living with my father's sister in Canada, I am once again alone in the house during the day. I remember my older sister playing with me during the school holidays. I liked that – I remember being happy. On one occasion we played dress-ups with all the clothes we found around the house, but we were super careful to replace them all exactly as we had found them. There is no telling what my mother would have done to us if she had known!

We also had three hula hoops someone had given us. We loved these and had great competitions as to who could make them circle the longest.

No-one else was in the house until we saw our mother arrive home around two p.m. Once Justine had returned to school, my life reverted back to doing the daily chores. I was now three and a half years old and much bigger and stronger, and more able to operate the mangle to squeeze out the water, before hanging the washing on the line.

"Susan, come here!" I dreaded that tone.

"We're going out into the garden."

Obediently I followed her out into the expanse of grass that defined our small, North London, garden. My mother was a good gardener. She loved gardening and spent most afternoons out with her plants. It was now nearly May and the weather was becoming warmer, and the days longer.

"You are to pull out all these weeds in the grass. Here. I'll show you how."

She then handed me a pocket-knife and showed me how to dig out one of the embedded grass weeds. There were thousands of these things! Each one was hard. They hurt my hands. I did it for hours! I was hot, thirsty, tired and sore, but no let off. If I slackened off, she came and swiped me with a stick, yelling at me to get them all out. So, get them out, I did.

Were there any thanks? No, of course not.

I learned early on not to argue with my mother and to just do as I was told. I learned never to let her see me cry and never to let her know that her actions caused me any pain or discomfort. I took it on the chin! I never flinched when she hit me – I just glared at her.

It was shortly after this incident that Justine and I became sick.

Loud banging on the door.

"Get this door open!"

More loud banging and angry voices.

In my delirium I could just open my eyes enough to see what was happening, and what was happening was too frightening to understand. Justine and I had both contracted Scarlet Fever, an illness at this time that was responsible for many deaths of children and adults. I was also diagnosed with double pneumonia, measles and whooping cough. Yes, I was very sick, but my mother had seen fit to leave us in that scullery room alone with no care.

I don't know what had prompted the action of the Men from Mars! Perhaps my father had surreptitiously made a call to the police (being too afraid to challenge his wife in person) or perhaps a neighbour had sensed something. I'm inclined to think it was my father, as behind closed doors no-one ever knew, or cared, about what happened in that house. The men who broke in that afternoon knew exactly what they were looking for!

I was terrified! As I looked around the room, there were many people charging about, yelling, and all wearing gas masks. One large, burly man picked me up from my makeshift bed and carried me out of the door. No-one spoke to me. The afternoon sunshine hit me full in the face, blinding me from the noise of people gathering to watch. Squinting through almost closed eyes, all I knew was – if the ambulance had a red cross on it, then I was safe. Looking at the vehicle I was being placed in – it was all white – no red cross! I passed out.

I have never been so terrified before, or have been since. Sheer terror shut down my body instantly. I had been awakened by the sound of people breaking down the front door, and then angrily charging in to collect my sister and myself. Wearing gas masks, I had thought they were aliens (not that I knew what aliens looked like). The isolation hospital at Hendon had a plain white vehicle, and as soon as I was placed inside the van, I felt as if I were falling down into a chasm of darkness.

"Wake up child," a nurse was tugging gently at my sleeve. "Your mother's here to see you."

It was dark outside. I looked around the room I was in and could see that my sister and myself were the only ones there. The isolation ward was on the top floor. The nurse took me over to the window where I immediately saw my mother waving frantically at me through the barred windows. I found out later that she had been refused entry into the hospital, and had become extremely agitated at not knowing where her children were. I didn't see her again for three months.

Justine and I liked it in the hospital. The nurses played with us and we had toys. We were also well-fed and could have a bath every day. Our clothes were clean. Since the time that I was born, I cannot recall feeling so clean, so happy and so like a child. When it came time for us to leave, we were upset – not just at leaving the nurses, but at knowing all the toys we had played with would be burnt.

We had spent over three months in this section of the hospital. It had been our home and at no time did we miss our parents.

On arriving home, I was immediately placed in a bed downstairs, but my sister was free to do as she pleased. At the time I thought this odd. In hospital we had both got up each day and run around the ward. We hadn't spent the days in bed.

"So now, why was I placed in bed?" I asked myself.

The doctor came each morning for a month and then I received a letter telling me he had died. My mother had read it to me. He had been eighty-five years old. (So, my mother had found a medic who could keep me in bed, because that's where she wanted me kept!) After that, I was moved upstairs, not to be seen again for eight months.

I once read a book, *Flowers in the Attic* by V. C. Andrews, which was supposedly based on a true story of a family who were kept prisoner in the attic of their grandmother's house in order for the grandmother to claim a family fortune. My mother kept me prisoner in one of the upstair's bedrooms from the time I was released from hospital in November 1954 to August 1955. The room was locked during the day but left open at night, when my father was home. No-one in the family came to visit me, except my mother who brought me tea, toast and two boiled eggs for breakfast each morning and tomato soup at night.

After breakfast, she gave me an injection in my thigh that really hurt, and then I slept all day. A potty was placed under the bed, should I need to use the toilet during the day. I do not recall ever having a wash, cleaning my teeth or having my clothes changed. My sheets were never washed.

It was customary for me to wake about midnight and then be awake until about six a.m. The nights were long, and I remember feeling such intense loneliness. The winter months were long too – in January it snows, and one can see one's breath in the cold night air.

My body endured this treatment until it could take no more. It was mid-summer. I could tell the changes to the season by the sounds of the birds outside my window. I know it was a Wednesday around three p.m. when my body finally said, "Get up!"

So, I did. I could hear voices downstairs and went to investigate. But – the door was locked. This had shocked me, because I had never attempted to leave the room before now. Being drugged from nine a.m. to nine p.m. gave me little opportunity to leave. I knew how to get out though. Justine and I had once played a game of hide and seek in which we had kept the key in the lock and used a pencil to dislodge the key and paper to collect it. The doors in this house were old, and the keys fitted loosely in the locks. It was easy to open the doors. It had been easy to open that bedroom door. (Perhaps that's why my mother was so angry when she saw me enter the lounge-room where she was entertaining her nursing guests).

I must have looked a sight. I would have been pungent, dishevelled and disoriented. As I opened the door, my mother's face changed from laughter to fury. She glowered at me, as she watched me walk into the room. Seated around the room were at least six of her nursing crones. She loved to make cakes and invite the ladies to eat them, which they did with gusto.

They all looked up and greeted me happily.

My mother didn't. "Get away from that trolley!" she had yelled, even though I was nowhere near the trolley. "Those chocolate biscuits are not for you!" she had yelled again.

"Oh, Jess, she can have just one," one of the ladies smiled at me.

"Don't you dare!" came the harsh voice again.

I didn't want chocolate biscuits, I just wanted company. Walking over to sit with a lady perched on the end of the table, I reached her just in time to catch the cup of tea she carelessly knocked over. The tea had been freshly brewed and very hot. I caught the cup instinctively, preventing much of the contents pouring onto the carpet.

"How did you do that, child?" the nurse had looked at me stunned. "Haven't you burnt your hand?"

"Yes, but it's all right," I smiled at her. "I'll go and get you some more."

I had then spent the afternoon chatting to this lady. Yes, I had burnt my hand, but with all the medication I had received over the past nine months, I scarcely felt a thing.

From that time on, my mother knew I could no longer be kept hidden away upstairs. School would start for me soon, and so I would no longer be a problem for her.

Or so she thought!

I wrote this poem for my daughter when she was struggling with her own issues. As mothers we are supposed to love our children unconditionally. At no time in my life did my mother show any care or love towards me.

Jewel Box

I wanted to let you know
That I love you.
I'm trying hard to understand
The little jewel box life you lead.
Your precious thoughts and dreams
Locked in your head
Are a treasure trove of riches
And little jewels that you need.
One day you'll open your box
And let them out,
So all of us can share these gifts,
And we will be so blessed indeed.

I've asked myself so many times how it came to be that two small children were left alone in a scullery kitchen while their mother went to work as a district nurse, caring for other sick or elderly people.

Why

Have you ever been so scared,
That when you close your eyes,
You fall fast into
A chasm of darkness
So black and so deep?
Have you ever asked yourself
Why it was you
Who was ridiculed
Or abused in this way
Each night before sleep.
And have you ever wondered
If there was a reason
You suffered that way.
But as you've grown older
You now understand
God's will and His commandment,
Just why you were chosen,
Just why it was you,
To give you the insight –
That's why it was planned.

It's because of these torments,
That your soul has grown strong
And taught you to help
All manner of others,
Who also feel pain.
So now as you guide them
And live life as you should,
In manner and kind,
No matter what happens – you'll
Still cy in the rain.

School Time

I turned five and started school. I knew where the school was. I had my lunch money and so off I went. No-one came with me.

For many years I was a Year Advisor in a girls' high school for Year 7 students. The parents always attended the first day assembly to make sure their children were safe and comfortable. When I think back on how anxious the parents were about their daughters starting high school, I smile as I recall the little five-year-old who walked a mile to the main road, crossed the busy highway and entered the school grounds all by herself. It was early, and there was no-one around.

The vast expanse of playground areas, surrounded by high brick buildings, seemed a maze of signs, pathways and doors.

Looking up to my left, I saw the 'kindergarten' sign and instinctively knew this was where I must go. So, off I trudged and sat on the steps outside the first of the three kindergarten classrooms. It was freezing, as I huddled in the warmth of the doorway, wrapping my scanty clothing around myself.

There was no school uniform in 'Big School.' The students could wear their usual day clothes. This was a problem for me because the only clothes I had were the makeshift curtains my mother had seen fit to alter to make me shorts and a jacket. From recollection, the curtains had been a heavy red and green plaid, that had hung on the windows for many decades. My mother hadn't washed them but had hauled them down and made as many outfits as she could from the three large panels. I had a jacket, matching shorts, a dress and a skirt. My underwear too, was made from the fabric, that was itchy and scratchy to wear. The shirt I was wearing was an altered one my father had long since had any use for.

In understanding my mother, one must understand a lady who never wasted her money buying clothes for her daughter. She didn't waste her money on food, let alone clothes. I was given lunch money because school dinners were cheap, and it meant I would not require food when I returned home at night. She did not care what I looked like, so long as it didn't cost her money to clothe me.

"Why are you here so early?" a passing teacher looks at me.

"I don't know. I was just told to come here," I look up at the lady, who was to be my teacher.

"Well, you'd better come inside. It's too cold out here."

I could tell she wasn't very happy. I sat quietly colouring in a picture of a cat until other children arrived with their parents. One girl caught my eye. She was wearing a beautiful cream, satin dress with a pink bow. On top, she had a pinafore. Hilary always wore a pinafore – even in Year 6. How I envied her.

I survived the day at school and returned home that night. *Would I survive my mother?* an instant thought attacked my brain, as I entered the backdoor of the house.

My mother was sitting by the boiler drinking tea.

"Well, what did you learn at school today?"

I knew not to answer questions like this one. I knew she was fishing for fodder to taunt me with, and I was right.

"Well, let's see. Here is a clock. What time is it?"

"Four fifteen."

"What time will it be in half an hour?"

"Quarter to five."

"How else can you say that?"

"Four forty-five."

In all my responses, I never gave my mother any emotive response. I simply answered her questions. She had been desperately searching for something to trick me with, and when she failed, she punched me in the head anyway. Getting up off her chair, she had been so irate, she had launched a punch to hit me full on my right ear, causing me to fall to the ground.

"You think you're so clever, but you can't fool me! When I was your age, I could knit my own jumpers – you, you're useless!"

She had then hauled me in front of a mirror by my pigtails and screamed into the glass, "Look at you. Look at yourself Susan. You're fat and ugly and no-one will like you!"

Her voice that day was demonic. When she said my name, I cringed. Even today, I cannot look someone in the face without remembering her harsh words. In Year 6, I was a school prefect and so sat on the stage. Facing the rest of the school, I would ask myself how these students could look at me. If I was so fat and ugly, how could they face looking at me? But they did look at me, and they did like me – so, had my mother lied?

Her taunts hurt, but I tried so hard not to cry in front of her. To let her see that her words affected me, would mean she had won. I had to win. I had to be strong mentally in order to survive emotionally. The more impact on me, the more pleasure my mother derived from her vicious ways – even at five years of age, I knew that that was her game.

It had been the following Saturday morning, when she returned from her district rounds, that I had been summoned. (I liked it when she wasn't in the house. She worked from nine a.m. until twelve midday on Saturdays, and I would happily clean the house in her absence. As soon as she walked in the door, I always felt I could cut the atmosphere with a knife).

"Susan, come here!" a harsh vindictiveness thundered the stillness of the air. Everyone froze when she entered – not just me!

Obediently I walked into the scullery room. Grabbing my pigtails, she then cut them both off. She then sat me down and cut my hair in a pudding bowl style. It had no style – it looked awful – I looked awful – now I knew I really did look fat and ugly!

I ran out of the room, out of the house and didn't stop until I reached the park. Here I found a large tree and buried my head in the autumn leaves. I cried for hours. When I returned to the house, my mother was watching television. She had bought herself a little TV the year before when they were first available. She liked her shows and loved to sit and knit at the same time. She didn't even look up as I entered.

"Susie, she did the same to me once," my father sat with me that afternoon. "I once foolishly let her cut my hair, but it was so awful that I had to stay home for a week until it was long enough to be cut by a barber."

Looking directly into my father's face, I said, "So why did you allow her to do this to me?"

I went to bed and cried some more.

She continued to cut my hair until I was thirteen years of age, each time causing me immense grief and significant loss of self-esteem and confidence. She had no skill in cutting hair, but she would never waste her precious money on allowing me a professional hair cut!

From the time that I can first remember, I have always looked after myself. No-one ever took any time to play with me or even supervise me. I was given jobs to do and just expected to do them. From as early as four years of age, I had a good sense of 'self.'

Finding Self

I've searched the deepest crevices
Of mind to find the inner me,
Exploring every nook and niche
With every boundless thought and dream.
I have the inner strength to reach
That span of body and soul
And delve into the deepest depths
In search of the essence of me.
I know the secret of all life
That many search, but few will find
Those hidden treasures of their mind.
I know what lies beyond the skies
That many scan, but few will see
The beauty that surrounds their soul.
I know what happens when we die
That many mourn, but few will feel
Their freedom spirit home and whole.
I've asked so many questions hard
In probing deep into my soul.
To find the richest jewels there

Swimming in oceans in my mind.
But now I can embrace myself
And as well the love of mankind.
Together sharing in this love
For all the universe to find.

Christmas

It's Christmas 1955 and what child isn't excited? I was excited. I couldn't wait, and like my two sisters, I had expectations of gifts. Christine was three, I was five and Justine was seven.

Just before my little granddaughter's birthday in December 2021, she had looked happily at her nanny, as they had sat painting pictures one afternoon and said, "Nanny, it's nearly my birthday. I'll be five, and then after my birthday, did you know, Nanny, it's Christmas?"

"Yes, I know that!" I had smiled back at her smiling, happy face. I knew she was excited to be turning five, because for her that also meant starting school. To all children that I encounter in my teaching life, they are hugely excited for their birthdays. They have parties, gifts, friends over and, of course, cake. I was too, before I turned five in October 1955, but that day I learned to dread any further birthdays. There was no party, no gifts, no friends over and certainly no cake! There was only abuse, castigation and punishment. "Why?" you ask yourselves. Because my mother could not bear to see me have fun.

On the day of my birthday, the abuse started at three a.m. when she hauled me out of bed to clean the steps outside the house. In late October, the weather is cold and often wet. That night it was drizzling rain, and I had bare feet.

"Why am I cleaning these steps when it's raining?" I bravely asked her.

"Because they need cleaning, girl."

They did need cleaning. They were caked in green mould that was difficult to remove with just a scrubbing brush. I also had nothing on my legs. I was wearing a second-hand nightie my cousin had given me, but that had only come to my knees. (I had no underwear on). I scrubbed for two hours. Finally, being allowed inside at five a.m. I had sat by the kitchen boiler to dry off. That was the first time I experienced chilblains. In later years, she frequently hauled me outside at three a.m. to clear away the snow, and I would come into the kitchen afterwards to nurse my itchy feet.

My father had wished me a happy birthday before leaving for work.

"Susie, I won't see you tonight because I have a meeting to attend. Have a lovely birthday. Your mother will no doubt have a gift for you from us."

Ah, so that was why she had deliberately chosen this day to taunt me. Her husband would not be home that night to know what she had done.

And go to town she did. I cannot relay the acts of degradation she inflicted on me that day, except to say that she wanted me to remember it for the rest of my life – and I still do!

But now, it's Christmas, and I do have an expectation of gifts. My father has asked for a tree to be put up in the hallway and he is excited. He can't stop talking to his three girls about Father Christmas coming. We all put up our stockings on Christmas Eve, sing carols and watch our mother open her mound of gifts. She always works in the mornings on Christmas Day, and so opens her gifts on Christmas Eve. I look at the mound. There are hundreds of gifts from her patients – they all adore her. There are also gifts for us from her patients.

My mother would sit for hours each Christmas and open the

gifts, carefully folding the wrapping paper. All gifts would be placed in suitcases, along with the wrappings, and stored under her bed. These gifts were the ones she then gave to other people on their birthdays or future Christmases. Unwrapping done, we all then went to bed to await the arrival of Father Christmas.

And he came…

I awoke at around one thirty a.m. when I heard my mother creeping into the room with a stocking to place on my bed. As she left, I looked across at the netting that contained a few nuts, a mandarin and a packet of crisps.

"This is not my stocking I hung up by the fireside," I say to myself.

(No, of course not – my mother was not going to buy us anything that was nice or special).

The nuts were walnuts that needed a cracking device to open, and the mandarin was stringy. The crisps were Smith's plain ones – I ate them.

As a parent, I always made Christmas special for my family. They always had stockings that they hung up and which were filled with wonderful goodies that they found beside the tree. Likewise, their gifts from Santa and Mike and I were always what they wanted.

Going downstairs on Christmas Day in 1955, I was, however, surprised to see three very large gifts under the tree. There were also gifts from relatives and my mother's patients.

"Susie, are you going to open your gifts now or later?" my father eagerly rubbed his hands together.

My father always called me Susie – I liked that. I knew I was his favourite. I was then and I remained so throughout his life. We shared a common problem – he was equally taunted by his wife, as future stories in the book will tell. He turned a blind eye because he did not know how to manage his wife's bizarre behaviours, and because he did not fully understand the extent of her abuse towards me.

Did my mother treat my sisters in the same way? No. She was initially jealous of me because my father always paid me more attention than he did her, and then later because of her three thwarted murderous attempts on her mother-in-law – she knew I was smart and so she set about knocking me down.

She totally ignored Justine – she paid her no attention whatsoever. Justine suffered from emotional neglect more than from any form of bullying or harassment. Justine was not a target for smacking or any other form of punishment. Interestingly, enough it was her favourite child, Christine, who was the target for smacking.

This is how disturbed my mother was. It was just before Christmas, after my birthday, when the first incident happened. It was a Sunday, and my father was at church. My mother came screaming down the stairs, "Who has ripped up this bible?"

She had then hauled Christine upstairs and smacked her for a long time. She was in a rage. The next incident happened a week later, again on a Sunday at about the same time.

"Who has wet the bed upstairs?"

Again, she hauled Christine upstairs and repeated her actions of the previous week.

I knew that Christine had not done those things. I knew because she had been with me in another part of the house. My mother had been alone upstairs. My concern then, and remained a concern for many years, was how a mother could commit such acts and then deliberately punish her child for them. "Was this something that happened to her as a child, that she wanted to play out as an adult?" I had asked myself.

Yes, I think that these situations happened in my mother's childhood, and she was blamed for them. Her mother was institutionalised for being insane whilst my mother was still a young girl. My mother was the youngest of three girls, and so was Christine. I was just glad it wasn't me!

What was hard for both Justine and I to hear, as we did often, was, "You know I don't love you. I only love Christine."

Justine and I would just look at each other and walk away. We knew what she was saying was true. I didn't care if she didn't love me – I just didn't want her hating me so much that I would not be able to survive her taunts.

"So, Susie, when are you going to open your presents?" my father's voice comes again.

"After lunch," I smile up at him.

We always had Christmas lunch. My mother knew she had to make an effort. It was nice. I always washed up. I would collect all the plates from the table and take them out to the sink. My father would help me dry the dishes, while my mother smoked her cigarettes. She was a chain smoker. She never made any effort to stop smoking, her excuse being that smoking kept away bacteria in her workplace.

I hated her smoking. I hated the habits that she developed because of her smoking. I hated the foul stench in the house, and I hated hearing her cough up her guts every morning. Of all the things this lady did – I hated her most for this habit.

Washing up done: "Susie, are you going to open your gifts now?" my father stands in the kitchen eagerly wanting his daughter to open his special gift to her. He has bought each of his girls the same gift, and he can't wait to see our faces when we open them.

No, I'll wait until 'she' has finished smoking, and then I'll come in. I then retreated upstairs for a few minutes. When I came back down, she just glared at me.

Our gifts were bears! They were gorgeous! They were huge – bigger than me. Justine called hers Julius Caesar, mine I called Brutus and Christine's was called Mark Anthony. We loved our bears and my father was very happy to see us so happy.

That was Christmas.

Well not quite…

It was a few days after New Year. Justine and I were still at home on holidays. My mother suddenly entered the house after her morning shift and grabbed each of the bears.

"I'm giving these bears away to more deserving children."

And without another word had whizzed them out of the door never to be seen again. We cried. My father had been livid when he had found out that night.

So, the following year, when my father asked me when I was going to open my presents, I just looked at him and said, "I'm not."

And I didn't. To me, while the gifts remained unopened, they remained mine. Even to this day, I do not open gifts when I receive them, always preferring to save them for a personal time when there's no-one around. I treasure every gift I receive. Sorry folks – I know some of you who know me think this is rude. Yes, it is, but I make no apologies.

An interesting parallel to this incident is seen in the book, *Mommy Dearest* by Christina Crawford, who was the adopted daughter of Joan Crawford, a famous actress at that time.

When Christina is a young child, she receives many lovely Christmas gifts. However, in the afternoon, her mother charges into the little girl's bedroom and takes all her gifts, yelling, "I'm going to give these to another little girl who is more deserving than you!"

Like me, Christina just sat and cried.

Having lost my bear that Christmas, as well as other dolls that I had been given as gifts from relatives, I never again placed any value on any item. I never allowed myself to become attached to any object.

Be Strong

My mind is so much stronger than my body,
Yet I remain its prey.
The slightest ache, or touch of pain
Still send me running to my bed.
If I am crossed
Or charged with wrong
I cower at these harsh words said.
I'm much too weak.
Why aren't I strong?
Why do I doubt what I can do?
I'm sure I feel the same as you.
If nothing else I've learned in life
That we all feel the need to share
Our weaknesses and inner fears.
My mind is so much stronger than my body
But now I've learned to stand up tall,
To tell myself what I can do
And cast disdain at fear and doubt.
I'll not be judged
By negative thought –

Instead, I'll stand and shout it out.
I've talents strong.
That can't be wrong.
I will not doubt what I can do,
And neither do I think will you.
If nothing else, these words I've said
Affirm what each of us can share –
Our pride and attributes so rare.

Mr Roundtree

New Year over and life returns to routine once more. At the beginning of 1956, would I have any idea what play or ploy I would become embroiled in? If I had known what was going to happen to me over the next few months, I would have left home. What happened to me savagely took away any capacity I would ever have to enjoy any sexual relationship with anyone, and more than that, it left me so confused about how a mother could so willingly do what she did – and for such personal, sexual gratification.

When I think back to the time, I was in the Hendon Isolation Hospital having nearly died from serious illnesses, to what I would now have to endure – no child should ever have to experience even just one of these episodes. Justine and I should have been removed from our mother. Why weren't we? The authorities barged into our house that day. They saw we were sick, alone and neglected. I shiver as I think what lies my mother must have told to convince the authorities she had good reason to not be in the house that afternoon when the police and health officials took us. At this time, though, it was believed that a bad mother was better than a foster family. How wrong were they?

Mr Roundtree was the gentleman who lived next door to us. He lived with his sister, who was in the habit of visiting her aunt on Sunday afternoons. She always left the house at one thirty p.m. and returned at five p.m. Her brother worked as an estate agent in the mornings and would stop off for a pint in the local hotel at around twelve noon. He would saunter home around one thirty p.m. after his sister had left.

This man was shortish, plumpish and baldish. He had a greasy appearance, and his clothes were baggy and unkempt – even when he wore them to work. In February, he devised a scheme to lure us girls into his house for the afternoon. He bought three packets of Roundtree's fruit gums – hence the name we gave him. These types of sweets are the ones you buy when you don't want sweets. No-one buys these – they are hard and horrible and get stuck in your teeth.

My mother had, of course, agreed, as she loved to spend the afternoons watching television and doing her knitting. It was perfect for her. Christine, however, refused to go. Even when, on one occasion my father was instructed to make sure we all went, she refused, creating a huge scene. He had relented and taken her back to our house.

So, it was just Justine and I who were privileged to go in and say 'Thank you' to Mr Roundtree. On the first occasion we walk in, he places me on his lap. He is wearing trousers and braces (straps) with a vest underneath. He begins by talking to us in sexualised language, words we have not heard before. He then begins fingering me, which makes me uncomfortable, and I squirm. He holds me so tight that I can't move and continues to explore that realm of my child body. Justine sits watching, not knowing what to do.

While he masturbates me, he begins to masturbate himself until he is satisfied and releases his hold on me. I feel the moistness in his groin and get off him at my first opportunity.

"I want you girls to do something for me," he speaks to us, and takes us into another room where three large bags of money lie against the wall. Glad to get away from this man's clutches, I move towards the bags.

"While I have a bath, I want you to count the money."

He then sets his bath in the middle of his scullery room and begins filling it with hot water. He spends the remainder of the afternoon soaking in the bath while Justine and I count the money.

He tells us, "I was involved in a bank robbery, and I got the coins. I need to know how much is in all three bags."

So, Justine and I set about sorting the coins. We get through one bag in the remaining time we had with him. We didn't mind it – we enjoyed it. We stacked up all the coins into crowns, florins, shillings and pennies. We said we'd come back and do another bag next week. We did.

It took us three months to sort and count all the coins. Each bag contained exactly one thousand pounds in differing denominational amounts. Each time we went, the man would wear less and finger me more. He would go further and make me masturbate him, again while Justine watched. Then one day, he sent me home.

Justine later disclosed to me what had happened.

"When he puts a board over the bath, you know what he is going to do, don't you?"

I nodded – yes, I knew. I had suffered this man's fingers for over three months, and I knew every sexual term in the dictionary. I knew what sex was all about, and I wasn't even fucking six years old!

After Justine had told my mother what Mr Roundtree had done to her, my mother did not tell the authorities, nor did she tell her husband or me. Instead, she saw fit to send me in – week after week. She would listen with a glass at the adjoining wall – I could always smell her cigarette smoke coming through the wall.

I cannot disclose what this man did to me each week. It is

vile, vulgar, lewd and crude and no child should ever even know of these behaviours, let alone be subjected to them. I would return home a mess each time and just clean myself up. My mother would dash upstairs as soon as she heard me coming in the backdoor.

On the day he got stuck inside me, I returned home in a terrible mess. I was bleeding badly and in terrible pain. I remember opening the kitchen door and vomiting on the linoleum. Of course, I cleaned that up before I cleaned myself up. I knew that my mother had been listening, and that she was now upstairs laughing at me. I could hear her cackling with Justine.

Being the good little girl that I was, I simply grabbed some tea towels to stem the flow of blood and went straight into the bathroom to run myself a bath. As I started to close the bathroom door, my mother waltzed in and glared at me. Her eyes were glazed over. She was sexually euphoric. I had never seen her like that before. I had seen rage in her eyes, but never sexual gratification. It scared me, and it was at that moment that I realised she enjoyed seeing me suffer. She got sexually high.

This same look I was to see many times in my childhood.

Removing my clothes, I stepped into the bath and slid myself entirely under the water. I did not surface for quite some time. I only surfaced when my mother grabbed me by my hair and yanked my head out of the water.

"Don't think you can ever tell anyone about this, because they won't believe you!"

These words had been said harshly and cruelly to me, and I believed her.

Sliding back under the water, I remained there for as long as I could before feeling my lungs bursting. I could not get myself clean!

I wondered what her next ploy would be.

Patience

In the aftermath of day
We reflect on what has passed.
Sometimes it's good,
But often we feel let down
By the people who don't give us
What we expect from them.
In the push and shove of life
We neglect the thoughts that count.
This isn't good,
As we let ourselves down
By losing precious moments
Of life's sweetest time.
In the early hours,
As we lie alone in prayer -
That's always good,
For those who listen to us
In this solitude and dark,
Will always be there.
In the final throes of death,
In the journey we all take,
We hope it's good,
And as we've listened closely
To life's lessons truly learned,
Peace and patience reign.

I have come to understand that my spirit guides are always with me. I can talk to them in the dark at night, or at any time during the day, and they will respond to me. This has been such a comfort in especially difficult times.

Wearing the V

"Susanna, you know we all wear the V, don't you?"

I look across at my friend, and she senses my confusion.

"When we suffer abuse, we wear the V sign," the lady continues. She then shows me what she means by placing her two fingers in a V sign on her forehead. "We don't see it, but others do on us."

"Yes, I guess. I've never really thought about that. Thinking back, though, I can think of many people who have looked at me differently, and now I know what they were seeing. When I moved to Cardiff, just prior to starting high school, I always wondered why the principal looked at me strangely. He was seeing my V sign."

We cannot avoid the scars. My issues with my mother created emotional scars, which for me were extremely difficult to come to terms with. My mother knew it. She knew I was clever – too clever for her to inflict physical harm on me. Physical harm provides evidence, not just of the assault, but also the confirmation that it happened. Psychological harm carries scars, but there is always that shadow of doubt about how much was really orchestrated or planned or even existed. So often in my life I've wondered if my reactions to my mother's taunts were really justified – could she really be harming me in this way? I always came up with the affirmative – but could never prove it, and so learned to wear it – and wear it I did well! Yes, I wore my V sign, but kept it well hidden!

My stories in this compendium are not designed to be entertaining or amusing in any way. My three previous books of sagas and poems* were specifically written as amusing, entertaining and very cleverly crafted accounts of embarrassing or interesting incidents that happen every day. In these stories I use many creative metaphors and similes, artistically articulated alliteration and assonance, witty puns that roll off the tongue and many other examples of language features to enhance the imagery of each situation. This is not what I intend to create in these stories. Many of the extremely difficult accounts contained within these walls would not want enhanced imagery. These stories are also not designed to shock people – that certainly is not my intention.

*The Lighter Side, Coffee Time – Come in for a Coffee and a Chat, Rags and Riches (Austin Macauley Publishing, London, UK)

My story is an arduous journey of survival. Each day my mother crammed as much insult, insinuation, instances of bullying, and instigation of taunts as she could to break my spirit, that by the end of each day I would be wound up so tight, my only release valve would be to scream silently under my covers. Even at five years of age, I refused to let her beat me.

For you, as readers, I perfectly understand those who will say, "These stories cannot possibly be true. They are far-fetched. No-one behaves as that mother did towards her child."

Well, they are not only true, but written exactly as they happened. When I wrote 'Tears on the Inside' in 2011, I chose to use the spiritual theme in which to embed my rationale for why these events happened. I am still of the opinion that this exclusive childhood barony, gifted to me, was an amazing opportunity for me to grow in spirit, and the reason I am now a practising spiritualist, and the reason I thank my mother for the part she played in developing my inner strength of mind and character.

There would be few people stronger minded than me worldwide – people who can withstand incredibly difficult situations and survive. (I had plenty of practice!)

When people talk about child abuse, they often do not differentiate between low-level and high-level situations. In our world today, we know to protect children, and by so doing see any level of abuse as deserving of attention and action. Throughout my teaching career I met many children who fell under the banner of child welfare services. I worked for two years each summer in a children's home that provided holidays for children who had suffered neglect or physical abuse by their families.

These children had my full attention, time, and empathy for the traumas they each suffered, but in the back of my mind there was always that nagging voice that reminded me that what I suffered was worse, but that I was never to use that gauge for any judgment purpose.

I remember the day the staff at the school, I was working at, were called to a staff meeting after school. We were being presented with the new Child Protection Strategy. I found this session very difficult to sit through, as it opened doors in my subconscious I had closed long ago. Listening to the instructions for reporting abuse, my skin began to crawl, and I started shivering violently.

"Fuck," I said to myself. "If this strategy had been in effect when I was at school, there is no way I could ever have reported my mother, and if anyone did report her, she was much too clever a liar to be charged, as was seen in her murderous attempts as well as when she left her children alone to die in that scullery kitchen.

In thinking this, I am reminded of a story I wrote in 'Coffee Time – Come in for a Coffee and a Chat' in which a young boy dies at the hands of his stepfather. In this situation, the child protection officers, counsellors and school staff were charged with neglecting to follow up on high-level incidents.

By the time the child was taken to hospital, he was so battered that his body could not take any more abuse. The nursing staff were distraught when he died and in disbelief that the system did not work. For the system to work, everyone must trust the people who have the power to act in the child's best interests.

In any of my situations, like this boy's stepfather who was believed by the authorities, my mother would also have made sure that she was believed. She was the master liar!

So, as I sat listening to the presentation that afternoon, I was fearful that there would be cases that would go under the radar – that the system would not, could not, will not always protect all children.

Child abuse is a serious crime. There are people who enjoy lauding power over children. It used to be a style of discipline when I went to school. There were teachers who enjoyed humiliating children in front of their peers. When I came to Australia, there were still teachers who used a cane to discipline boys – never girls.

Many people wrongly assume that teaching girls is easier than teaching boys – but in my fifty-five years' experience in the classroom, I disagree with this assumption!

So, why didn't the girls get the cane?

In writing my story, many readers have commented on how sad it must have been for me to endure such a loveless and heartless childhood. Yes, it was, but at no time after I left home was I sad. Even as a child I tried so hard not to reflect the negativity on the outside that I felt on the inside.

Sadness

Sadness wrenches our hearts
Releasing energy
That helps us heal our hurt.
Sadness grips at our soul
Allowing us to feel
The pain of life and strife.
Sadness enhances light –
Renewing energy
That gladdens heart and soul.
So have patience with sad
And weather stormy times.
Release joy in your heart
And know you have the strength
To face the wind head on
With courage and vigour
To once again, feel trust,
In all you do
To gladden heart and soul.

1956 and Just 6

Susanna was now accustomed to her life and what to expect. The one thing she had learned so far was, 'not to expect!'

In her first year at school, she had seen many children excitedly rush into the classroom on the days of their birthdays and proudly display their assortments of 'show and tell' gifts they had opened that morning. Susanna had envied them. They were happy children and their parents obviously loved them. These girls had lovely dresses, clean knickers, shoes and socks to die for and ribbons in their hair.

Susanna looked down at her hessian clothing and second-hand plimsolls. It would soon be her birthday. Gosh, how she dreaded that day. At least this year, she was going to be prepared. "I have to have a plan," she announced to herself the day before. "I know, I'll get up around three a.m. and walk into Harrow. It will be dark, and no-one will see me. I can sit in the park and then hide in the school grounds until eight a.m.

Our house was over two miles from the laneways that led down to the parklands. I never minded being out alone. I found it comforting and the walking distance gave me time to think and relax. As a child I became used to walking for miles each day. It was always the best therapy. I knew where the fields were that housed horses, and where the blackberry bushes sprouted their delicious fruit. Many houses had fruit trees, which in October bore glorious fruit. I could usually scrounge an apple or two.

The night air was cold, though, and I shivered intensely as I crept out of the house. A chilly wind nipped at my neck.

"Where do you think you're going?" a deep, voice resonated behind me. "Get back to bed this minute!"

I turned around and glared at the voice. "How did she know?" I cringed, and then cried out as she whacked me across the face.

Plan A thwarted, I lay in bed frantically trying to think up another plan. *I know*, I thought, *I'll just get up around five a.m. and do these jobs she's going to make me do any way. That way I'm in control of what I'm doing, and she can't be cross because I'm doing them.*

And so, I did…

I went outside and cleared the leaves from the pathways, swept out the shed and washed the tiles leading to the outhouse buildings where the laundry and toilet were. I cleaned the toilet. It was filthy! It was six a.m. by the time I came inside and began clearing the ash from the fire grate. My mother had taken to burning anthracite in the old, open fireplace. It made the room warm at night, but very dirty around the walls and ceiling areas, as well as the grate. I was filthy!

Hot water was not usually available in the mornings because the boiler was never lit during the night. I was used to washing in freezing cold water. There was an outside tap near the toilet where I stripped naked and scrubbed away with the carbolic block that was called soap. It didn't look like soap, it didn't feel like soap, and it didn't clean like soap, therefore it wasn't soap!

But I felt cleaner! All that scrubbing and enduring the freezing tap water, made me impervious to the outside air temperature of 5° Celsius. I then took some mouldy bread from the pantry, laced it with dripping and ate it on my way to school, just glad I had at least survived this first part of the day.

School was the usual, until…
"Happy Birthday to you,
Happy Birthday to you,
Happy Birthday dear Susan,
Happy Birthday to you."

The whole class clapped and cheered. I couldn't believe it. (I never told my mother!)

One of the mothers had made the cake and wanted to surprise me – well she did! It was Hilary's mum. Hilary remained my friend until we left primary school at the end of Year 6. Hilary was very good at English, and I envied her ability to write stories. She also went to tutoring on Saturdays. Her mother knew I was envious and bought me the same book Hilary used in the sessions.

Now I could walk up to the tutor's house on Saturdays and sit outside and do the same lesson Hilary was doing with her tutor. On Mondays we would then sit together and mark our work. I loved these times.

I think it's why I like being a private tutor for primary children now. For young children to be nurtured in this way is wonderful. To have an adult help them with their reading and maths is wonderful. My students now, in my current life, love their sessions with me. They feel so special.

It was the Sunday after this birthday that the force-feeding episodes started. (Had she found out about the birthday cake, and was it this that had prompted this food taunt?) I couldn't fathom it. Suddenly, after lunch, she was forcing me to sit and eat mounds of mashed potatoes and peas. At first, I didn't mind, but when she kept forcing me to eat more than I could stomach, I became physically ill.

"Why was she doing this to me?" I asked myself. The rest of

the week I knew there would be no food. When I was allowed to leave the table, I went and sat in the outhouse toilet and cried until the pains subsided. That took four hours. When the stomach is stretched beyond reasonable capacity, the pain is excruciating, and it lasts until most of the food has passed through. It was incredibly cold in this outhouse, and the draughts whistled around my scrunched-up body. I sat and hugged that freezing cold, porcelain and not very clean toilet, as if it were my best friend.

Each subsequent Sunday was the same. It was the third occurrence when I could stomach the pains no more and remembered being told once, that if you put your fingers down your throat, you can vomit. I did. It worked. I didn't feel full, and the pains went away. I felt empowered.

That afternoon I realised that it didn't matter what that woman did to me, all I needed was a counterattack. As soon as my mother realised, I didn't care any more, she stopped – she wasn't going to waste good food on me!

What scared me most, was knowing the lengths this woman would go to, to destroy me. She had tried to hurt my grandmother, she also taunted her husband and she targeted me. When I saw the glassy-eyed look in her eye, each time she succeeded in hurting me, I knew she was getting self-gratification from her taunts.

"So, what's next on her agenda?" I asked myself.

It wasn't long before I found out.

As a little girl I cried myself to sleep every night, cowering under the bedcovers with my fingers in my ears to shut out the outside world. I would press down so hard on my ears that at one time I did damage to my right ear. I couldn't tell my mother because that would have disclosed my secret habit, which she would then have exploited.

I'll Cry a River

I'll cry a river for me
Every day that I live –
Every hour that I spend,
Every second of time
My tears will flow strong – for me.
I'll cry a river of tears
For the love that I crave,
For the time that I'm brave,
With their moments of bliss
So precious and few – for me.
I'll cry a river for life,
For the pain that I feel,
For hurt that won't heal.
For no soft, gentle touch.
My tears will flow strong – for me.

A Slap in the Face

1957 and I'm in Year 1 at school. Having turned six towards the end of the previous year, I was now expected to do more of the heavier types of chores, such as lifting heavy furniture or changing the sheets on the beds. Changing sheets always meant turning the mattresses, and always without help. I would then move the beds away from the walls to clean under them and around the skirting boards. I never once saw my mother lift a finger to do any housework!

It always seemed to me that she devised these jobs just to keep me busy. Fortunately, in the winter months, the garden work did not need to be done, but for some reason the house furniture was required to be moved from room to room.

"Susan, take this wooden table into the hallway. I want this lounge moved into the room next door, and then bring that lounge in here."

I once had to move a wardrobe downstairs. After emptying the contents, I thought I was really clever to lie the wooden cupboard on its side and slide it down the stairs. The stairs went straight down, and so did the wardrobe. I laughed, it looked so funny. I was glad my mother hadn't seen it!

The weekends were difficult to bear. Even at this very young age, that curtain of gloom would descend upon me around two thirty on a Friday afternoon. I would find myself slipping into a sombre mood and go intensely quiet. In high school one Friday at this same time, I remember a teacher asking me why I was walking with my nose on my knees. Straightening up, I had looked at her and said, "Oh, I'm sorry, I hadn't realised I was."

I became so used to this veil of gloom that my whole body would slump forwards and I would look towards the ground. By fourteen years of age, this postural position had become quite pronounced, but I hadn't noticed it.

The entire world looks forward to weekends. They make plans. They have fun, family times. They go shopping or out to dinner. They ride bikes or go to the park. I dreaded weekends and knew I had to make plans to survive them.

Friday night I would stay at school until five p.m. and then walk the long way home, getting there around 5.45 p.m. My mother would be watching her television and smoking her cigarettes as she knitted. She would be leaving for her hospital job soon, and so I only had an hour to endure. Friday nights was my bath night, so that night was covered. Apart from acknowledging her as I entered the house, I could steal away upstairs and lie in the bath until she'd gone. I would then wash my clothes and hang them to dry in the kitchen.

Saturdays were difficult. I didn't have many escape routes during the times when snow lay icy on the roads and pavements. It was too dangerous to walk too far. Not able to sneak to my tutoring sessions outside Hilary's tutor's house, I would do the lesson at home in the mornings. With my mother at her district nursing job until noon, I usually knew I was safe to use the scullery table to sit at.

On this occasion, my father had decided to sit with me. We had both had breakfast together and then vacuumed and dusted the house. It was ten a.m. when we sat down with our tea and work. He had some accounting tasks to do and really enjoyed this special time with his favourite daughter. He liked me because I was smart. I was smart. I knew that. I learned my lessons at school easily. I could read and write in Year 1.

Suddenly, the front door latch was heard. We both looked up, as my mother thrust open the scullery door and stood staring at us. (She must have suspected something and deliberately orchestrated to catch us at it – whatever that 'it' was!)

"How dare you do schoolwork in this house!" she ranted.

"How dare you waste your time doing that rubbish!"

She then yanked the English coursebook from my hands and began tearing it into tiny pieces.

"Ha!" she cackled. "Now see how you like your precious book now!"

My father had just sat there staring at her. He did not know what to do or what to say to her.

"Now, get upstairs and vacuum the stairs!"

I faced my mother and quietly said, "We've already done the stairs, the hallway, bedrooms and living rooms."

I did not flinch or move a muscle as her blow caught me full in the face.

"Don't you dare be so insolent to me!"

I left the room as my parents argued bitterly that morning. It was my guess that she had suspected we were spending time together on Saturdays and was insanely jealous of the attention my father gave me.

The whole world wants their children to do well at school. Every parent I have ever known has urged, encouraged, coaxed their children to do homework at home. Me, I was happy to do homework – any schoolwork at home – but now this delicious way to spend time was denied me. From now on I knew I would have to sneak up to the library - but I had lost my workbook. How would I get another one? For me it literally was – 'a slap in the face!'

My mother had gone back to work after that incident that morning and had not returned until two p.m. when she cooked the usual liver, mashed potatoes and cabbage. I would never eat the meat, only the vegetables, something my mother didn't mind, as it was more for her. Sitting at the table, she had sat bolt upright and faced me.

"Susan, from now on you will spend Saturdays with Mr Morrison."

"Who is Mr Morrison?" I looked at her with no emotion on my face.

"He's a famous actor who is willing to give you lessons on Saturdays."

That was all she said. The following Saturday the address and how to get there were given to me, and I was just expected to turn up on his doorstep, which I did.

The door had opened, and I was shown into the first room – a reception room. The house was huge and beautifully furnished and decorated. Mr Morrison did not speak but showed me around his house. I don't know what he was expecting – certainly not a six-year-old wearing curtains for shorts, a second-hand sweater with moth holes that didn't fit properly and holey plimsolls.

What struck me about this man's house was that every room was furnished in a different colour and era in time. I was too young to know about periods in history, but I could tell the difference between furniture that was modern and what was antique. My father had many antique pieces of furniture as well as trinkets that dated back to the early 19th century.

There was no doubt this man had made money from his acting, but I didn't know who he was, and quite frankly – I didn't care. I would much rather have gone to Hilary's tutor's house and sat outside in the cold to do my English work.

The man made me tea. When he spoke, he had an affected voice, and I suspected he was a homosexual. His body language was feminine and gestural. He was nice to me, and we made a television commercial for Polo Mints. He had all the equipment set up in a special room – I felt so special! I loved it! OMG I loved it! I couldn't wait until next Saturday.

I knew that Mr Morrison was one of my mother's patients. At first, I was confused why I was going to his house. He hadn't needed to teach me how to act or make commercials, but on the third visit I did find out.

The ploy had been to get me to shower and change my clothes into costumes he had set ready for me. By this visit, I felt comfortable in his presence. On the second visit, he had cut my hair, something I was immensely appreciative of, as my hair was a disaster most of my childhood. So, now I trusted him.

Once I had showered, he had entered the room and taken a shower himself. I had seen a naked man before – Mr Roundtree had taken a bath in front of Justine and I. Mr Roundtree had looked disgusting naked, but this man was lithe and fit – stunning to look at. I suspected he had cancer, though, but his body showed no signs. I remember being entranced by this man, until…

Yes, here we go again. I wondered if my mother knew this man was a paedophile. He was clearly gay with a preference for little girls I presumed! I never went back.

Sundays were not so difficult to bear. After church we had lunch and then my mother would do her sewing. She had a little sewing area in her bedroom and would hide away until five p.m. If the weather was not too cold, I would sneak out and walk into Harrow and play in the park. If it was snowing, I would read my books I had borrowed from the library. Sunday nights were early bedtimes, and then a whole glorious week of school. The weekdays were bearable – I had my survival strategies all worked out and they worked – I could survive these times. Going to bed at night, I could breathe a sigh of relief and relax a bit.

But not that night!

Obviously, my mother had found out about Mr Morrison and so it was time for punishment.

Hang on… I did nothing wrong!

When I look back at the times my mother had psychotic episodes, I think they were associated with a type of personality disorder that she had. During the time that I lived in her house, I saw four quite distinct personalities. I cannot say she had an obsessive, compulsive disorder, or schizophrenia because her condition went undetected and so untreated. What I can say, is that she was fuelled by jealousy. She was intensely jealous of me, and so any time she saw my father giving me attention, could possibly have been the trigger for one of her psychotic episodes towards me.

It was the Sunday night after the Mr Morrison incident. I had not disclosed to her what Mr Morrison had done to me, but I had talked to my father about why I wasn't going back there. He had stared at me that afternoon, and again, had not known what to do or say to his wife. He knew my mother had a serious mental problem, and yet did nothing about it! (He must have told her, though!)

Sipping my tea in bed that night, I began to feel woozy. I just thought I was tired. As I drifted off to sleep, I felt a strange dissociative feeling in which my mind and body seemed to separate. It scared me, but I was too deeply subconscious to fully realise what was happening to me. It had been a few hours later, after I had been sleeping, that I felt as if I were in a dream, and someone was beating down upon my back with a stick. I always sleep on my front, and I had a blanket covering my back and shoulders. The pounding was a frenzied attack on my person that lasted long enough for her to hit me at least twenty times.

This woman was clever. If she had lunged at me in the cold light of day, she knew I would have reported her to someone. There would also have been the physical evidence of the assault. Hitting me so viciously in my drugged state, and with a blanket covering me, she knew would not leave such marks, nor would I be able to prove she committed such an act.

After she had finished, she had quietly left my room, never to mention the incident to anyone. If you have ever been drugged like I was that night, you would know how frightening it is to not be able to connect your brain to your body. It took four hours for this reconnection to occur to a point where I could begin to fathom what had happened. Getting out of bed that Monday morning, I felt so stiff and sore around my back and shoulders, and my head hurt very badly.

Making tea and taking Panadol, this assault had been more than 'a slap in the face' for me. It affirmed my mother had no respect for me now or would have in my future.

I was fucking six years old! She cut my hair, stole my bear and took my dignity!

How dare she!

Courage

Have the courage to live your life
By giving to others and knowing what's right.
You have the strength to stand up tall,
To face the challenges and give life your all.
Be not afraid to reach beyond
The boundaries of life - you've potential strong.
Believe in yourself. Your strength of mind
Will help you overcome the toughest times.
Be pure in thought and kind in deed,
Then measure your success by what you achieve.
Before you know, such joy you'll find –
Happiness so strong in body and mind.
Lift your head high – smile at the world.
Then people will see your beauty unfurled.

Healing

Heed the advice of others and
Enjoy the newness of day.
Allow yourself the time to dream and
Love yourself, I say.
Is it comfort that you want?
No-one is free of pain – so
Give yourself the biggest hug
And smile – that's nature's way.

Anyone for Gym?

Jim was Tuesday nights. Jim had returned home from his prison stretch. He had been incarcerated for stealing cars. I have no idea how this situation *evolved*, and I do not want to know! All I know is – it *involved* me!

"Susan, you have been invited to go over to Jim's house tonight."

"Who's Jim," I asked taking no interest in the conversation.

"Jim has just come home from working in the army and needs some company at night. He would like you to go over and chat to him on Tuesdays.

So, off I toddle and find that Jim is the oldest boy in a family of five boys. He is eighteen years of age and hasn't found a job yet. His mother, father and four brothers all live in the house I front up to. (Of course, Jim hadn't been in the army – he was too young for one thing. He had, of course, been in jail).

Jim opens the door and takes me into the hallway where he asks me to do handstands.

"Why do you want me to do handstands?" I ask Jim.

"Because your mother said you were good at them."

So, I do handstands. I do handstands every Tuesday until I discover that Jim has been arrested again – this time for an indecent assault on a young girl.

So, I don't go again.

Thinking about this situation later in life, I seriously ask myself how a mother can deliberately send her little six-year-old daughter into a stranger's house to do handstands for an hour a week? I didn't own gym wear. I had no decent shorts. I had no decent underwear! This boy would pull my legs apart and stretch out my legs and then teach me how to do walkovers. I was quite good. He taught me how to do the splits and how to push myself backwards into a piked splits. I enjoyed it – I was then and was all through school – a good gymnast, but...

I was starting to see a pattern in my mother's thinking. "Did she know what I was going to be doing, or was she just trying to be helpful to this family?" I ponder over this notion.

Jim never touched me, he only looked. He certainly did that! There were no further sexual episodes until I was a teenager. I'll relay these two here, rather than record them as separate teenage issues.

The next encounter happened when I was in Year 8. My father had changed his job, when I was twelve and we had moved to Cardiff, Wales for twelve months. We only returned because my mother hated living away from London. I really liked Cardiff. I loved walking by the river and exploring the castle. Returning to Harrow, however, meant a better house for us. It also meant my mother only worked as a district nurse in the mornings, giving up her hospital shifts. This man in this first incident, I discovered later, was one of her patients.

My best friend at school was Lynne. Lynne lived with her mother about a mile from our new house in North Harrow. I went to Lynne's house most nights. Her mum would make me dinner and we would do our homework and chat in her room for hours. I loved this lifestyle. We both did well at school and so helped each other with our essays.

It was walking home one night that was the problem. I had walked about half the distance when I sensed someone following me. As I turned the corner leading to my street, a man grabbed me and pinned me against a wall. He placed both hands on the wall above my head, and, thought that he had me cornered. Not so…

I say this to girls all the time. Martial arts give you great self-defence skills for two reasons:

1. The perpetrator is likely to be male, and not expecting you, as a female, to have skills.

2. It is instant self-defence. Self-defence skills give you the confidence to know how to assess a situation, and to know how and when to act.

In my assessment, my body was free. He thought that by placing his hands either side of my head against the wall I could not escape. How wrong was he? As soon as he made a move to kiss me, I brought my right knee up into his groin, which made him bend at the waist. I then linked my hands together, put them behind his head and slammed his face into my rising knee. This made him fall off-balance and break his nose. I then used a trip throw to bring him to the ground where I could put my right knee into his right clavicle, dislocating his ball and socket joint. The whole manoeuvre took less than six seconds.

The owner of the brick-walled house was a police officer, who called an ambulance and took me home. My mother had been kind and thankful to the policeman but had only glowered at me. I had made a statement and the man had been sent to prison after receiving hospital treatment.

It had been two years later, when I saw the man again. My father and I were travelling back from London. We had just stopped at Harrow on the Hill station and were progressing to North Harrow. A passenger, who had just got on, turned to sit, and then just stared at me. I began to shake as I stared back at him.

"Susie, what's wrong?" my father had looked worriedly at me and then at the man. He sensed something was very wrong.

I didn't tell him. It was the man who had assaulted me.

Catching up with the police officer a few years later, I discovered the truth.

Yes, of course my mother had known – and had orchestrated it as she had done the next situation.

This next incident is recounted in my book, *Rags and Riches*. It is written in third person directive.

Susanna is fourteen years old and home alone. There is a knock at the door.

"Hello Sue, can I come in?"

A middle-aged man is smiling at Susanna's front door. He knows her parents are overseas and that her younger sister is out.

"Yes, of course. Can I get you some tea?"

"Yes, that would be lovely. Thank you."

As the young girl puts the kettle on, she wonders why the school counsellor from her school is visiting her at nine p.m. She looks at the kitchen clock, as it strikes the hour. More pertinently, she wonders why one of her school friend's father is visiting her. Her friend, Barbara, is in her class.

"I somehow don't think Babs knows he's here. This situation seems odd to me," Susanna worries as she takes the tea into the lounge area.

"Sue, I've come to talk to you about a project I want you to be involved in," the man begins nervously.

Susanna listens attentively, but senses something is not quite right. Her suspicions are founded when the man begins to move into her space and forces himself on her. Had he not been her friend's father, she feels she would have struck him. She also feels that, had he not been the school counsellor, she would have struck him, or at least attempted to throw him off her. This man was very large, though, and at least double her weight and strength. In her pinned-down position, there was little she could do until he had finished.

When he had, she had simply said, "I think you should leave."

(She never told anyone – until now).

She was, however, certain her mother had instigated it in some way. This man had been expecting me to be compliant. At six years of age, I could not have conceived that my mother would deliberately plot these ploys for her own sexual gratification. Later in life, however, I saw many bizarre behaviours that made my skin crawl when I think how any person could be capable of committing such atrocities.

Mental health disorders are complex behaviours that require a professional diagnosis and medication treatment plan. I saw many obsessive, compulsive behaviours behind closed doors. If others saw such behaviours in their interactions with my mother, they did not make any move to help her. She worked with medics! They must have seen something!

This woman must have been hungry at some stage in her life. I never had any food to eat, except bread and dripping, and yet every cupboard, larder, washing machine, wardrobe, bedside table, display cabinet, attic space would be filled with tins of fruit, baked beans, packaged foods, dried foods, cans of soup, sugar, flour and treacle. She would send me to the shops each day to bring back more tins and then have me squeeze them into any available space or bury them in the garden. We never ate any of them. (She probably did dig up the buried ones when we moved to Cardiff!)

A future incident in this book describes a situation in which she forces me to go shopping – I'll say no more!

Empowerment

Empower your head to search and find
Your deepest thoughts of inner mind.
Empower your heart to love yourself
And rise above the push and shove.
Empower your legs to walk with pride
And grow in strength with every stride.
Empower your feet to raise you up
To see beyond the highest wall.
Empower yourself from head to toe
And affirmation you will know.
Empower to stand for what is right –
Now all your dreams are in your sight.
Well done!

Police Business

Rap, rap! A very loud rapping was heard at the door.

Looking up sharply from her knitting, my mother said, "Now, I wonder who that can be?"

I was sitting quietly in the scullery outbuilding peeling and slicing green beans, and I looked up sharply. No-one ever came to the house at night. It was dark and well into the evening. I asked myself the same question. The unusualness of the encounter aroused my interest. My mother went to open the door. My father was probably in his room with his headphones on. His escape at night was to listen to his music. I immediately jumped down from the chair and crouched behind the scullery door, leaving it open just enough to see who was making that rapping sound. What I saw and heard aroused my curiosity, bringing a wry smile to my face.

"Madam, I'm Police Constable Peters and this is Sergeant Harris from Harrow Police Station. We'd like to ask you a few questions.

I couldn't believe what I was hearing, and I couldn't believe the response I saw from my mother. I had never seen her go so ashen white before. Listening furtively that night, I wondered what offence she had finally been caught doing. A string of incidents flooded my mind:

1. *My grandmother's incidents.*
2. *The isolation hospital episode.*
3. *Mr Roundtree's Sunday assaults.*

4. Mr Morrison's Saturday assaults.
5. Jim's inappropriate gymnastics.
6. Stealing from shops.
7. My absences from school.

In considering the stealing episodes, I was hoping it was those. I had been with her on many occasions when I saw her steal items. She would never buy anything in a shop if she could avoid it. She had to buy food, but this was only ever essential items, or food for storage purposes. The only household products she bought were carbolic soap and vinegar. I had to use both of these to wash my hair with.

To clothe her children, she had initially removed all the curtains in the house to make into as many outfits as she could, including underwear. As we grew bigger, she became accustomed to sneaking into haberdashery shops to browse the materials, sneaking remnants into her bags, always retreating from the premises without being caught. "Well, was she now caught?" I asked myself.

Another stealing practice was to scrounge around the jumble sales. She didn't mind us wearing second-hand clothes from these outlets, especially when she had secured 'freebies!'

"Susan, you go and distract the lady while I find some things over there."

I knew what that meant. She would then grab me hastily and fly out the door with her stash of goodies, hoping to go undetected, which she always was. *Or perhaps not!* I thought to myself that night.

I was frightened. Although I knew my mother did bad things, I didn't want her going to prison. I didn't know why she did it – we weren't poor! My father's ancestors had been upper-middle-class. My father's father was a personal, friend of the writer,

Charles Dickens. My father was an educated man and now worked as a senior accountant for British Rail, having passed his exams. My mother wasn't poor – she had two jobs! As a young child, I was always so confused why we had so little. The people in our street once gave us toys they didn't want any more, my mother's sister sent us clothes her children had outgrown and some of my mother's patients gave us sweets occasionally.

"Why couldn't she buy us the things we needed, like everyone else's parents did for their children?"

I was still in Year 1 at school, but soon to be turning seven and in Year 2. Over the summer, Christine, a girl in my class, had invited me to her house one afternoon for tea. Christine came from a working-class background. I knew that when I went to her council house. Inside it was so much cleaner and more 'homely' than our house. Her mum sat us down in the kitchen and gave us a boiled egg, toast and little cupcake. We drank orange juice from a glass. It was wonderful – I loved it – I was treated kindly.

Her mum had said, "Darling, we don't have much, but what we have we happily share."

Christine's father had then walked me home.

"We can't have you walking home by yourself," he had smiled at me.

Why not? I thought. *I do every other day!*

Now, listening at the door, what would I hear?

"You'd better come in," my mother's voice sounded shaky and unsure, as she led the two officers into the main sitting room and closed the door. I now couldn't hear what they were saying unless I ventured closer.

Was it my absences from school? I thought. Ever since the Saturday morning, when she ripped up my English workbook, she had begun keeping me home from school. I knew I was good at school, but as soon as she realised this, her ploy was to prevent me doing well. She kept me home and told the school I was sick.

I hated those sick days. I never knew when she would charge into my bedroom in the early hours of the morning and yell at me to get out of bed and go into the spare room (the one that had been my grandmother's). Here I knew what she would do – it was always the same. She would punch an injection into my thigh and leave me alone to sleep through the day. I missed so many days of school like this. Every year was the same, even in high school. On one occasion the principal of my high school came to the house to find out where I was. I had been off for three weeks. Of course, seeing that my mother was a nurse, the principal believed everything she was told, even giving my mother permission to keep me home for another three weeks!

Cowering behind the living room door, I shook my head, "No, it's not the school absences. She always sent me back to school with a note."

"So, what was it?" I keenly listened. It was a juxta positional moment: on the one hand I was scared to death and yet on the other, quite excited!

The police officers' voices were loud and clear. I had no trouble hearing the conversation. My mother answered their questions nervously at first, but then I could feel her voice and manner relaxing as she understood the reason for their visit. She even began giving them that fake laugh of hers, the one she used when she wanted to impress people.

"All right, so she's not being arrested?" I surmised, partly a little disappointed. Part of me believed my mother should be held accountable for her actions, even though part of me was hugely relieved when the police officers finally left.

"Mrs Makeham how well do you know the neighbours on

this side of your house?" one of the officers asks my mother as he points to Mr Roundtree's house.

"I know the lady. She helps me with my children sometimes," I hear my mother say.

I think, "That's a lie! She has never helped us!"

"Are you aware of any inappropriate behaviour from these people?" the second officer asks his question.

"No," my mother had simply said.

"Another lie," I say to myself. "She knows about the money, and she knows about the rapes!"

"Have you been into their house and seen any possessions you might have considered suspicious?"

"No," I never go next door.

I wondered, "How can my mother lie so blatantly?" I could not believe my ears. I had told my mother about the money and how much Justine, and I had counted. She had known about Justine's rape, and then sent me in to be raped! If she had thought I was lying about something, she would have smacked me silly, and yet here she was deliberately lying to the law!

I had told her that Mr Roundtree accounted for his three bags of coins as being his proceeds of a bank robbery. "Did my mother think, that if she dobbed Mr Roundtree in, the police would find out about Mr Roundtree's other crimes?"

Yes, I think she knew it was best to keep quiet, and so she did, quietly showing both officers out of the door. I had then hastily retreated to the scullery as soon as the policemen made a move to leave and pretended to continue peeling the beans.

"Why are you still up? Go to bed this instant," she screamed at me.

I obediently took myself off to bed.

Lying in bed a short while later, I knew I couldn't ask my

mother any questions about the police officers' visit. I also knew I couldn't tell my father. If my mother had known I had listened, I couldn't imagine what she would have done to me. "So, what should I do?" I asked myself as I drifted off to sleep.

On waking, I knew exactly what to do. Throughout my life, I have always had my questions answered in my sleep. I know it is my spirit guides who guide and steer me through my life. They look after me, protect me and give me direction.

After school that day I called in at Harrow Police Station and told them about the coins. Of course, I didn't mention anything else.

"How dare you! How dare you go to the police station?" my mother had swiped me the next day, when she found out.

I learned early on in my life never to show my mother any emotion. If I cried in front of her, it would have been fodder for more insults. If I became aggressive towards her, then she would have taken to me with a stick. The only way to win with her, was to show her no signs of any emotional response at all – nothing, which is what I did, however hard it was. When my eyes were bursting to cry, and my heart felt like lead thumping so heavily in my chest, I learned to just stand there and look directly at her with no expression on my face.

Mr Roundtree (real name Mr Jones) was arrested and sentenced to twenty years in prison. He only served five of his sentence, passing away from a heart attack.

On hearing the news that day, I had cried tears of relief!

The recounts in this book are all true accounts of incidents that happened. In laying bare my life, will people see me differently? Will they judge me? When writing my initial story in my book, 'Tears on the Inside' I was conscious that, by disclosing very personal information, people might be shocked, or even appalled. The friends I had at that time were amazed that I had experienced such a difficult situation, because I appeared to them to be the most normal person in the world. And yet, how can I be normal when I have experienced such an abnormal childhood? (Therein belies the truth!)

Truth

I never mean to tell the lies that fall too often from my lips.
I'm really, not untruthful, yet these lies lie ready on my lips.
What can I say when truth is hard and often brings such sorrows sad.
Such small white fibs can mean less harm, so are they really all that bad?
I've always said, "Be true to self" and rest each night with conscience clear.
By telling tales I carry guilt that leaves me crying many tears.
So now this New Year as I make a resolution I can keep,
I'll go to bed each night and know the field of Earth is mine to reap
Be true to self and stand up proud - this new-found honesty's my goal.
With conscience clear I'll face the world – self-confidence has freed my soul.

The Angel of Mercy

Harrow is a prestigious North London satellite town sixteen kilometres from London. It's notoriety stems from the existence of the highly elite, private school known as Harrow, a school where England's Prime Minister, Sir Winston Churchill was educated.

The post-war decade saw Harrow rebuild its wealth and prosperity quickly, with many professional people commuting to and from the big city every day and establishing middle-class incomes and lifestyles.

My family was this family. My father commuted to London on the tube train each day, carrying out his business lifestyle oblivious to the lives his children were living.

"Was this an advantage to me?" I had asked myself many times during my formative years, particularly when the children from working-class families seemed to have more than me – more food, clothes, shoes, toys and love – not much of which I had.

My father was a successful accountant, but one who spent most of his days at work, or attending cricket matches during the summer months. His wife, my mother, was the 'Angel of Mercy.'

The entire town revered this wonderful lady, who spent her working days caring for the aged or palliative and who was extraordinarily good at her job – a facet I witnessed first-hand when I accompanied my mother to work on many occasions as a teenager,

So, why was this seemingly well-off, middle-class lifestyle not conducive to my happy, loving and successful pathway through childhood? And why, and how, did I become so acutely aware of the juxtaposition that existed in the way my mother lived her life. By the age of seven, I had seen two quite distinct personality shifts. I had seen the happy district nurse who couldn't do enough for her patients to the very unhappy wife and mother who could, or would, do nothing for her children, or her husband.

Was it because she wanted to impress her patients? She saw no point in impressing her family. Yes, that's exactly how I saw her persona. When anyone came to our house, she was always keen to impress them, impress them with what she could make, what she could do, what she had achieved in her life and in feeding them as many cakes as possible. Yes, these people all listened attentively to my mother's boasts, happily stuffing themselves with chocolate cake. Of course, there was no chocolate cake for her children.

So, it was understandable that people did not realise what was happening in our house. Only people from poor backgrounds got abused – never people from middle-class homes! (I encountered this perception many times during my childhood. Here is one such occasion).

It had been a Wednesday morning at eleven thirty a.m. I'm in Year 2 now and it's early October. My birthday is at the end of the month – not a date I wanted to look forward to. I'm standing in a line waiting for my work to be marked by the teacher. In front of me is Brenda. The teacher takes this girl's book.

"Oh, my goodness, Brenda!" the teacher exclaims. "Just look at your hands!"

Brenda began crying and explained to the teacher that her mother made her scrub the floors each day before going to school.

"I'm going to have a word with your mother," the teacher looked crossly at Brenda.

I looked at Brenda's hands. Yes, they showed signs of having to do hard physical labour. She had callouses on both hands and blisters from all the scrubbing. I didn't dare look at my hands, for fear the teacher saw mine. In handing her my book, I kept my hands well hidden – but I needn't have bothered – she wasn't interested in my hands – I was from a middle-class home and so there was no thought given to any work I might have to do at home. Brenda – she was working class and so a cause for concern.

Sitting back down in my seat, I surreptitiously looked at my hands – they looked far worse than Brenda's. Of course, they were, I'd been scrubbing floors since I was two! I put my hands away.

No, behind closed doors in our house, no-one knew, no-one cared, and no-one took responsibility for reporting anything that went on there, even though I did discover over the years that people did become suspicious.

After my mother passed away, I went to the house in London to get it ready for sale. I met with the neighbours who lived to the left of our house. The wife had been a court administrator all her working life, and her husband had been a barrister.

"Susanna, we both knew strange things happened in your house. We both recognised that your mother was a bit odd," the pair looked across at me as we sat sipping tea.

"And you never thought to report her?" I looked sternly from one to the other. "That was always my problem – people knew but chose to do nothing! I was fucking six-years-old!"

And I don't excuse my language – I have a code when I write that indicates my level of anger in relation to the context of the information relayed.

I use the 'f' code when I am moderately annoyed about a situation, or when there is also a modicum of humour associated with the absurdity of the situation.

I used the 'f _ _ _ code when the annoyance is greater and warrants greater stress on the inappropriateness of the events being relayed.

I use the fuck word code when the situation is beyond reproach because what has happened is not acceptable in any walk of life.

I use the f _ _ _ _ _ code when a situation is savagely wrong, and I use the full word when it goes hyperbolically beyond the realms of decency and acceptance.

What happened in the first Harrow house went beyond comprehension and what occurred throughout my teenage years in the second Harrow house, leaves me with lifelong scars I can never remove. Anyone of any of these incidents that spanned sixteen years of childhood would likely impact as mental health issues for many people. I'll talk more about these teenage years in later stories.

This story relays situations that depict the type and level of emotional abuse my mother chose to inflict upon me. Whilst there were certainly episodes of physical abuse, not because parents were not supposed to hit their children at this time – they were – it was considered 'good parenting,' these physical assaults were defined actions that I could recognise as incidents. I knew I never deserved to be punished physically. I never did anything wrong. I couldn't – I had to be above being naughty. I always knew that if she hit me when I didn't do anything wrong, what would she do to me, if I did? From the time I awoke in the morning, I was always on my guard for any sign of something my mother was going to do or get me to do. I lived on my nerves! No, the abuse she directed towards me was emotional – she was out to break my spirit. I just never knew when she would attack.

"Get up!

Get out of bed. You've been there long enough!"

As she yanks the bedcovers off me and drags me physically out of bed, I am aware that it is the middle of the night and freezing cold. It's January 1958. Overnight it has snowed, the reason my mother is prompted to drag her small child out of her warm bed in the middle of the night to clear away the snow.

I have no shoes on or socks. My scanty nightwear is inadequate for the freezing temperatures of an English winter. My mother watches me shovelling snow, that has accumulated in the driveway, from the warmth of the front lounge room. I can hear her laughing and see her smiling at me through the windows. I knew she enjoyed seeing me suffering in this way. Whilst the work was fairly difficult for a young child to do, I always knew the impact on me was more emotional. She was taunting me. She didn't want the snow cleared, she just wanted an excuse to belittle me. This situation happened several times in my life. I learned to always be on my guard.

Returning to bed I nursed my frozen feet. I wondered if I would get frost bite. I hated the chilblains because my feet itched and ached for days. As I drifted back to sleep, I hoped she wouldn't bother me again that night.

She didn't – she had other plans for me that day.

It was a Thursday and Polling Day – so no school. Polling Day in the UK was conducted on Thursdays and students had the day off school, because the polling venues were schools. I walked up with my sisters and my mother to the local school and waited while she voted. We then all walked home again. Everyone she met embraced her, complimented her, revered her! She was the town's 'angel.'

"Girls, you are so lucky to have your mother," one elderly lady smiled down at Justine, Christine and myself. "Your mother does such good in the community. We all think she's a saint."

She was a saint to her patients. I knew that. How my mother loved these conversations. I saw a happy, smiling, relaxed lady enjoying the attentions of those who greeted her. As soon as we walked into our house, I saw a total change in her disposition. She was anything but happy and relaxed.

"Susan, come here!" my mother's voice carried an edge to it.

It was always me – never either of my sisters. They both just did as they pleased.

"I've made a shopping list. Here's some money. You are to go and get these items now."

As I traipsed off to the shops, I asked myself why we couldn't have bought these items on our way home from voting. She wanted flour, sugar, treacle, golden syrup, tins of fruit, tins of soup – all highly unessential items – and all very heavy.

Thursdays was my mother's baking day. It was her day off and a day when she usually had the house to herself. She made rock cakes, a walnut loaf and a malt loaf. If she knew she was having visitors anytime soon, she would make a trifle and a chocolate cake. So, I obediently went to collect items I assumed she needed for her baking.

It was a good mile walk to the nearest shops and took me about twenty minutes. There were no supermarkets at that time, only the corner shop and the specialty food stores, such as the butcher, baker, confectioner and grocer. All my mother's needs could be purchased in the corner store today, which is where I went.

Walking home, the bags became heavy. My plastic bags bulged and knocked against my legs. My arms became tired from the weight of the tins and pounds of flour and sugar. Thankfully, I arrived home safely and delivered them to my mother.

"Now, here's your next list."

I looked at her list this time. She had written a whole page of items, including bread, potatoes, marrows, carrots and turnips to name a few – all heavy, bulky things. Again I wondered why we all couldn't have carried these things home earlier.

So, once more off I trudged. Walking to the shops was no chore. Going into all the different shops was an inconvenience. Working out how much money to give each shopkeeper was not really a problem, - I was used to going shopping and buying things. I had good money sense and skills. Carrying the goods home became the problem. I had reached the midway point – the section where the mainroad gave way to an alleyway that led to our section of town, when I just couldn't walk any further. My arms ached too badly and my fingers bled from the thin plastic handles that bit into my flesh.

I rested for about half an hour before being able to continue. When I finally did arrive home, I got yelled at for taking so long. I hadn't expected to go out again!

The shopkeepers all saw me go into their stores three times that day. They saw how tired I was becoming, and they saw how much I struggled to physically carry the shopping home. None of them made any move to help me.

This time she wanted a pantry load of tins, dried foods and

eggs. Having filled up six bags of heavy, bulky items, three bags on each arm, I seriously wondered how I was going to get them home. I tried every way I could to carry the bags without making my fingers bleed more. The grooves in my fingers had become swollen, red and bleeding quite badly. I tried putting one bag over my shoulder, but the plastic handle just broke, spilling out the eggs that all smashed onto the concrete. I sat and cried. I couldn't go home without the eggs, and I had no money left to buy more.

"Darling, what's the matter?"

I looked up and saw a kind lady peering down at me.

"You're sister's daughter, aren't you?"

I nodded and then explained what had happened. "Please don't tell my mother."

I must have had a really, frightened look on my face, because the lady jumped back quite startled.

"No, no, of course I won't. I'll go and buy you some more eggs."

I was so grateful. I sat and waited for her to return, which she did with another plastic bag. It was now getting quite late in the day and drizzly rain was beginning to fall. Picking up my bags once more, I headed home just glad that no-one could see my tears in the rain. There were many times I walked out when it was raining, so no-one could see that I was crying.

I knew from the onset that my mother had not wanted the shopping. She had seen an opportunity to bully me and cause me grief. She deliberately chose the bulkiest, heaviest items she could think of to make me buy and carry home.

Walking in the rain that afternoon washed the blood from my fingers, making them sting. This was my life and I had to survive. I couldn't even let her know she had got to me! I couldn't let her see my fingers or give her any indication the tasks she'd given me to do had in any way caused me pain. I knew she had emotionally bullied me.

With the sun now gone and darkness creeping over me like a foggy blanket, I was thankful no-one saw my tears.

Throughout my childhood, I had always wondered why no-one said anything to the authorities. The police officers who removed my sister and myself from our house, when we had Scarlet Fever, and had been left alone to die, had not taken any action against my mother, the police who notified my parent's about the ceiling collapse in my grandmother's bedroom had never investigated the matter, and none of the people I encountered at any time I lived in Harrow – people who saw that I had no clothes or food, or that I was walking the streets in the dark, ever raised any alarm.

Blindness

People look without seeing.
They listen without hearing
All manner of senses,
Misunderstanding their meanings.
People think without knowing.
They touch without feeling.
These senses not telling -
Interpretations gone missing.
People talk without speaking.
They move without talking,
They are caught up in hectic
Realisation left sleeping.
People wake without living.
They take without giving.
Their greed and their selfish
Extinguishing life's memories.

Living the Tornado Life

When you're eight, nearly nine, you know what you want, you know what you can likely expect to get, you know your place in the family and most importantly – you know your place in the world!

My place in my family was unimportant to me. I knew quite clearly that I was my father's favourite – he called me Suzels, or Susie, and I knew I was smart. He wanted me to go into theatre acting like his cousin did. (His cousin had been a notable actor, having a key role in the film, 'The Windmill Theatre,' which received much acclaim at the time, as did he as one of the leading actors).

No, my calling, right from the time I was born, was to be a teacher. I knew this was my place in the world. At school I taught the students to do gymnastics, to ride bicycles and to shoot hoops in netball. My prized possession, a gift from my father, was Billy Ball – my real leather netball.

Billy and I were inseparable and a source of much dialogue between us, particularly on cold, wintry mornings when I would arrive at school around six thirty a.m. We would amuse ourselves and keep ourselves warm by shooting goals, Billy always trying to stay out of the hoop and me trying to get him in! I always won! I went on to become the Goal Attack for my school netball team. (I also went on to play netball for North Wales).

I didn't need other friends – I knew this then and I know it now. I'm here to help people, particularly children – I am not here to be distracted by social nuances, however nice it might be to share a glass of bubbly whilst watching the ocean on sunny Sunday afternoons. Ah, such chagrin! But, at eight to nine years of age in my house, my life was a tornado. Each morning, from the time that I was yelled at to get out of bed – usually around five a.m. in freezing cold air conditions in which, even in summer, one could see one's breath in the air, my nerves would begin to spiral as every second wound them up tighter.

Most mornings the bed covers would just be ripped off me in a callous and uncaring way with a snarl to get up. I always obeyed, as I knew Billy was always so keen to get up and out too. Washing in freezing, cold water was something one gets used to. It wakes you up!

So does trudging through snow in less than suitable footwear and rainwear. Once at school, though, everything was all right. Life for me like this was a way of life I could live. If I left early, before my mother had even made her first cup of tea, then she couldn't decide I wasn't going to school. Keeping me from attending school was something she did regularly. She was determined that I should not do well at school.

My mother only had time for my younger sister. Christine was to be the one to excel – like she did, or so she said she did. (I have my doubts!) Christine, however, was not as smart as me, and neither was my older sister, Justine. My father recognised that I had academic ability and encouraged me to find secret ways to study. He never knew about my school absences, and I couldn't tell him for fear of retribution.

It was only when my mother began pushing the idea of nursing into my head, that I saw an opportunity to attend school more regularly.

"Susan, you will be a nurse when you grow up."

This had been said to me as a fait accompli, not as a possible option. At first, I had argued with her, stating quite firmly that I was going to be a teacher.

"You! Teach! Don't be ridiculous child! You'd be a useless teacher – you're not smart enough! The students would hate you. They wouldn't even be able to look at you, you're so fat and ugly!"

She had screamed these words at me with such venom that day, that I could stand the stress and disappointment no longer and left to cry in the dark. She had told me I was to be a nurse since I was two years old. She never saw any other option for me. I became fearful that I actually, would have no choice later in life. That terrified me, as I was so aware of how dominant and obsessive she was. I never met anyone who couldn't do exactly as she said. If her nursing friends did not want a piece of cake, she made them eat three large slices!

The next day, though, I saw the light. I'd play her game. I'd lead her to believe I'd take up nursing and then try and change this later in life.

"If I'm to be a nurse, then I need to be at school more often."

This was said to her as a fait accompli! (Yes, at eight to nine years of age, I was learning!)

Accepting this fate, and driving my own agenda, put me more in charge of my days. It put me more in charge of my life.

Back at school in that cold and draughty playground at six thirty a.m. I didn't mind being alone. I liked school, so did Billy, and by eight a.m. Billy had lots of friends.

Home time was the biggest challenge. Where could we go until it was dark? Once a teacher asked me what I was doing in the playground at five p.m. She had sent me home. That was then ruled out as an option.

Going to the library was always a possibility. This was an hour's walk from school and at least half that again back to my house. Walking became a good way to unwind the spiralling tornado. I would walk for hours arriving home most nights around six thirty p.m. At this time my mother was usually watching television and wasn't bothered by my appearance. I would forage around for something with as little penicillin mould on as possible to eat. Bread and dripping with marmite, was always a good choice, as were the stale rock cakes that could be soaked in tea to make them more palatable to eat.

And so, weeknights were manageable. Going to bed at night I would pull the covers up over my entire body and head, stick my fingers in my ears so that I would not be able to hear the sounds of the house, and then scream silently until the tornado had unwound enough for me to survive another day. (I cannot divulge the stressors that built during each day that wound me up so tightly). Even to this day I have a very severe inability to manage external noises – my nerves simply cannot cope – the man who sniffs, the lady who picks her teeth, the clicking sounds that some people make with their teeth, the fidgety, nervous tics that anxious elderly people acquire – all set my nerves into overload.

As I grew older, I became more aware of my mother's behaviours, not because I hadn't noticed them before, but because I was so confused by how different she appeared to all my friends' mothers. I was invited to friends' houses – I saw how loving and kind they were – I saw how well-dressed and well-fed they all were, and I saw how much they all enjoyed spending time together. My family never spent time together. We all spent our lives trying to avoid each other.

I did, however, begin to look closely at how my mother interacted with other people. I became an observer of her idiosyncrasies. Even to this day, I am fascinated by human behaviour. It intrigues me why people do what they do – what drives them!

My mother was driven by an obsession to appear to be the best, not just in her job, but in everything she did. It was almost as if she had to appear to be incredibly strong to the world to prove herself. *What happened in her childhood to drive this agenda?* I thought.

"Susan, when I was three, I knitted my own jumpers! At five, I made my own dresses. In Year 6, I matriculated with honours!" And so on and so on…

She would rant for hours to me about how wonderful she'd been in her previous life, as a child, as a teenager and as a young adult. I was never good enough for her. I could never compete with what she said she had achieved. No matter what I tried to do, it was always fodder for criticism and castigation.

In considering my mother's behaviours, I don't care now, and I didn't care then, if she'd been the best at anything, all I cared about was trying to survive her behaviours that impacted on me. She subjected me to substantial sexual abuse, that did not stop when I was eight to nine years of age; she abused me physically whenever she felt like it because she knew that at any point in any day, I feared that punishment at any unguarded moment; she neglected to provide my basic needs physically and emotionally; she imposed slavery and imprisonment on me and humiliated me beyond the realms of normalcy and societal acceptance. Her subjugation methods controlled my thoughts, deeds and words to a point in time when I would hit that breaking point and make the decision to commit suicide. (That's a later story!)

I suffered immeasurable emotional abuse, that no words can describe (and I'm a good writer!) In my life, I have tried not to be the 'victim' despite wearing the 'V.'

Observing my mother's behaviours, it became clear to me that she had a multiple personality disorder. She was also obsessive compulsive. I would see her sneak up into the attic late at night to hoard large quantities of food, none of which she needed – there was ample already stored in the washing machine, the shed, every cupboard and wardrobe in the house and in suitcases under her bed. I would see her sneak out into the garden in the middle of the night to bury food. (She must have been hungry at some point in her life?)

I knew this behaviour was not normal.

I too, have a level of obsession. Mine is about cleanliness. At eight to nine years of age I cleaned the house every day. No-one else did. Certainly not my mother. I was, and still am, fastidious about floors.

In my current life, when my little granddaughter was four years old, she said to me one day, "Nanny, I have heard people say that you can eat off the floor in your house. Is this true?"

"Yes, why do you ask?"

"Because I've just dropped a lolly, and I want to eat it."

"It won't kill you to eat something off the floor!" I laughed at her serious face.

"I know Nanny, but I don't know where the floor's been."

"It hasn't been anywhere – it's just been here."

"Noooo, Nanny, it's been in the woods!"

Yes, my floor is made of wood.

"Yes, I know, but I've washed it since!" I again laughed.

"Nanny, have you never heard of that expression?"

"What – to be 'in the woods?'"

"Yes," she cackled.

"Yes," I cackled, "I'm just surprised you have!"

I was floored!

As a child I was always hungry. There was never any 'real' food to eat. Much of what I ate contained penicillin mould or was stale, like the bread and rock cakes that lay around for weeks. Dinner at night was never provided for me.

My most favourite social pastime in my current life is sharing a meal with someone, especially dinner, and especially a meal that I have prepared and cooked for my guest.

Fear

Have you ever been hungry?
Have you known what hunger is?
Have you felt the void of emptiness
So deep down in your soul?
Have you ever been lonely?
Do you not know solitude?
Have you heard the cry of silence
Screaming in your soul?
Have you ever been frightened?
Have you sensed the smell of fear?
Have you seen the light of darkness
Shining in your soul?

My Suspicions

In 1960 I turned ten, weighed ten stone and stood 5'4" tall. I was a young adult. I behaved like an adult and people treated me like one. Now in Year 5 at school, I worked hard to be the best I could be. Never being allowed to do any schoolwork at home, I was in the habit of spending most of my time at the library, which was always open until eleven p.m. weeknights and until six p.m. at the weekends.

I loved reading. I also loved writing. When I discovered that the best way to unwind the tornado inside me, was to write how I felt, I would write myself copious notes and then tear them up.

My parents argued incessantly each night, another reason to stay clear of the house at these times. My father suffered from my mother's abuse. She belittled him – said he was useless and criticised him constantly because he was not a handyman. No, he wasn't, he was an academic. She hated that he spent his evenings listening to music. He loved the classical pianists. When he passed, he gave his whole collection to my husband, Michael, who also enjoyed spending hours with his headphones on.

Unlike my mother, I did not mind Michael listening to his music. Michael was a musician. He wrote and played a variety of musical pieces for piano and saxophone. Some of his pieces were published by schools for use at assemblies and special memorial days.

It was around November when my father came to me quite unexpectedly and said, "Susie, if your mother and I get a divorce, will you live with me?"

I didn't know what to say. What could I say?

The next day, my mother was standing in the kitchen with her back to me, when she said, "You know you are not to live with your father, if we get a divorce!"

Again, her words were a fait accompli. There was never any negotiation with her, and I knew my father would never win against his wife. He never had, and now certainly wouldn't. If she made plans to have her children, then that's what she would do. (I suspected that it meant she kept the house!)

It was about a week later when I suddenly heard loud shouting coming from their bedroom. It was a Friday night. He had come home late. (I suspected he was having an affair with his secretary).

The next morning my mother informed us that our father would be leaving on the Monday. No more was said on this topic all weekend. On the Sunday night, he packed.

"So, why is he still in bed on Monday morning at eight a.m.?" I asked myself.

After my mother had left for work, I went in and asked him. I knew I too should have left for the day, but I couldn't leave without knowing what had happened. He had really, bad flu that had come on suddenly. My mother had been so annoyed her plans had been thwarted! He was sick for a week and then was well enough to return to work. No more was said on the matter. My father was a weak man – he had chickened out!

Returning to work also meant resuming his affair, an affair he continued to maintain for many years. I met this lady several times. She was lovely and totally devoted to my father. She was also respectful to my mother when there were occasions when they found themselves in each other's company.

As Christmas loomed, my mood gloomed. I could cope with weekdays, barely coped with weekends but holiday periods were significantly difficult times. The Christmas period usually involved four days when everything closed, and then there was the New Year break when Harrow shops remained closed, even though the London sales commenced on New Year's Day. I was so glad when my father came to me and said, "Susie, I've noticed you do not have a jumper. Here is ten pounds for you to go and buy one from C & A in Oxford Street."

Wow! I thought. *Yay!*

I immediately set off for the train. I didn't need fare money, as I was afforded a free travel pass on trains because of my father's job. It was wonderful to travel into London by myself. I knew how to ride the underground tubes. I knew all the colour-coded lines, and I revelled in watching all the assortments of people who travelled in London over the Christmas period. There was snow on the ground, but the trains were warm.

Sauntering along Oxford Street, I browsed the shops and delighted in this little escape for the day.

In C & A I selected a beautifully soft, fluffy white sweater that fitted me perfectly. I loved it and was so happy with my choice.

So was my father. He was so proud to buy me something I wanted and liked so much.

Was I allowed to keep it?

No, of course not!

"Where did you get that?" she attacked me instantly I walked in the door wearing it.

"From C & A."

She was ropable. She was beside herself with anger.

"How dare he give you money for such things!" she ranted.

"Take it off immediately!" she screamed.

"I don't have any jumpers! I have nothing to wear! He bought this for me – not you!" I let rip.

"You have that Fair Isle one I knitted for you," she almost thrust her face into mine.

"Yes, when I was five. It doesn't fit me any more," I continued to rip. (She had once collected all the odd scraps of wool she could from a charity shop and knitted me a jumper, that at the time I was grateful for, except the changes in wool thread, combined with the stitching styles, made it tight to wear, and somewhat uncomfortable – not to mention how it looked, which wasn't good – but at the time was a jumper).

"You ungrateful cow!" she scowled at me and launched a whack to my face. "Take it off!"

My father had been livid, but his wife had won - the jumper disappeared never to be seen or worn by me again. (I suspected she gave it to one of her patients!) The next day she presented me with a bag of black wool, knitting needles and a pattern.

"Here, if you want a jumper so much, knit one!"

I did. I wore it every day, including to school, until I left home eight years later. (I suspected that my mother had been secretly annoyed that I had been able to knit such a successful jumper, as she never said anything to me about it).

My jumpers now are my prized possessions. I select them very carefully and keep them for years, making sure every pair of jeans or leggings matches perfectly with each of them.

Her next ploy, I suspected, was deliberately designed to get back at me for buying the jumper and then knitting my own so successfully.

"Susan, it's about time you earned some money," she flew into the kitchen one day and announced.

"But I'm too young," I replied, a little taken aback.

"No, I've checked. You can do babysitting. Here, go to this house this afternoon and look after their child for the night."

I obediently fronted at a house in Ruislip, which was a train ride from Harrow Station, and then a twenty-minute walk. Going there presented no problems, as it was light, but walking back to Ruislip Station had no streetlights, and then home from Harrow Station was uncomfortable, as people looked strangely at me. It was eleven p.m. and very dark walking down the alleyways.

I babysat for this family for about six months while the wife was studying and taking her medical exams. Her husband was a doctor, and the pair had decided it was easier to study at the university library, than with their one-year-old at home. After the wife had passed her exams, the babysitting stopped. I never received any money. (I suspected that my mother did!)

The next babysitting job I did was for nine months.

"Susan, you are to be home every Friday by five p.m. because Jacob will be here."

"Why am I required to look after him. Why doesn't Justine – she's older than me?"

I was annoyed that I had to be home on Fridays because it contradicted my survival plan. Being in the house at night was not easy to tolerate my mother's chain smoking, continual coughing, ticking noises that she made or her sudden outbursts of temper. The only good thing about Jacob being there was that there were sandwiches. She made us sandwiches and tea to eat and drink while we played various games. Jacob was all right. He was a little Jewish boy, different from the boys at my school. I liked him and he loved playing the games we played together. He never wanted to go home when his mother came to collect him.

Jacob's mother never said thank you to me, though. (I

suspected she thought my mother looked after him. I know she paid her money!)

My next job was looking after a young girl who had leukaemia. The first time I met Clarise was when her parents invited me for tea one Saturday afternoon. Everyone was lovely to me. I was happy to look after her on Saturdays while her mother went shopping. I would arrive at two p.m. and leave at five p.m. Clarise had no hair, and she was very pale. I knew that her prognosis was not good, and so I felt immensely sorry for her. She wanted tutorial sessions, something I wondered about. When I asked her one day, she said, "I just want to be the best that I can be."

I smiled at her that day and thought, *Yes, me too!*

We had lovely times, but once again, there was no money for me. (I suspected that there was for my mother!)

Once Clarise had passed, my next patient was an elderly lady of eighty-five. She just wanted to die and would keep on at me to get the doctors to give her something. My job with this lady was to wash her and then her clothes. I would also cook her eggs on toast to have with her tea. Her death came suddenly and unexpectedly. I arrived at the house as usual and let myself in.

The lady was lying in bed, still breathing, but could not speak to me. I immediately went next door to ask the neighbours to call the doctor. I had come to know all the doctors my mother worked with, and they were always friendly and helpful to me, even if they did expect me to do things I wasn't supposed to do, such as give medications.

I had sat with this lady that day and had felt her peace. When she slipped away, I was holding her hand. I felt the warmth drain from her body and said a prayer for her.

To Gladys,

> May God take your hand and guide you
> As you leave this world behind.
> May you feel the gentle whispers
> In the breezes of the wind.
> May your thoughts be safe in Heaven,
> May you wake to bright sunlight
> Where never will you feel again,
> Such sorrow from Earthly pain.

Watching Gladys die did not frighten or appal me. I had seen a dead person before. When my mother's father died, we all had to trek out to the crematorium to see his body. She made me kiss him. He was so white and so cold, and his skin had a soft, plasticky feel to it. It didn't look real.

I wasn't overly concerned about not being paid for any work I was doing. I enjoyed going to people's homes because it was so much more fun than being in mine. My next job took me to Hoover factory in Wembly. This job was a filing clerk for three hours a night, three times a week. I have no idea how my mother got this job, I suspected one of her patient's sons worked there and needed someone to keep his paperwork in order. I started at six p.m. and finished at nine p.m. At this time of night, no-one else was there.

I would open the door, that was left open for me. Upstairs there was always a mound of papers on various desks. I would sort them all into piles according to types:
- Invoices awaiting to be sent
- Payment vouchers for employees
- Letters

- Receipts
- Orders for goods this company wanted to purchase
- Staff meeting notes
- Miscellaneous

I would then catalogue each item in a ledger book before filing it away in the cabinets. The man I worked for liked my work. He said he had never had such an organised office and that he particularly liked the ledger entries, as he knew exactly what had been filed away and when.

But…

The job stopped suddenly. I suspected both he and my mother had been 'sprung!'

Finding Peace

We all have many paths to take.
May the roads rise high to meet us
As we walk on life's highways.
May we find around each corner
A trove of wondrous praise.
If we make the right decisions
Every time paths twist and turn
We'll find that realm of inner peace
We've longed for all our days.

Shine

Be not afraid of who you are
Or who you want to be.
Allow yourself to love someone -
It'll set your spirit free.
Be proud of you for what you are -
It'll let your light shine through
Be sure to keep your heart and soul
As pure as pure can be,
For if you do, your loveliness
Will shine eternally.

The Pragmatist

I feel a little like the reporter who wrote the Anna Sorokin story – the story about a young girl who posed as a wealthy German heiress to deliberately scam wealthy socialites and big banking corporations into giving her millions of dollars in cash. This story is incredible, or rather incredulous that these famous people and high financiers fell for Anna's ploys – but they did! My story, too, seems incredulous that any human being could be so broken themselves, that they sought to inflict such harm on another human being.

As I have grown older, I have come to realise that my mother's own childhood must have impacted negatively on her. Another film I remember watching, (I rarely watch films!) was the story of a child who savagely had her sexual organs removed in a vicious and callous way, leaving her mentally scarred and with a multiple personality disorder. I feel that some devastating act was inflicted on my mother in such a way that it disturbed her psyche, resulting in her experiencing at least three different personality moods and a severe obsessive, compulsive disorder.

The reporter on the Anna Sorokin story reached a point in her research when she just had to sit down and write the story. This is how I have felt in writing my story. So many facts have gone round in my head, I haven't known where to begin, or the order to relay events, or whether I am really remembering what happened correctly – like Anna's journalist, she puts off and puts off the writing until…

She just has to sit down and write.

And me too - I just had to sit down and write.

I am a pragmatist, though, and have a behavioural approach to how I manage all aspects of my life. This means I am a realist. I see the concrete details and determine that all behaviour must be accountable. My mother was never made to be accountable for any of her behaviours, largely because no-one really knew, except me. Those who suspected, turned a blind eye because my mother was so fiercely dominant that she could never be challenged by anyone.

As a nurse, working a district nursing round, as well as a night shift in a hospital, she worked with many medics. I would have thought one of them would have picked up on a behaviour of concern. Considering the elderly doctor, she engaged to manage my jaundice when I was four years old, certainly did not challenge my level of sickness, instead giving me exactly what my mother asked him to provide for me. Did he just want the money?

Over the years many medics came to our house. They saw my mother behaving strangely. Was it, that at that time little was known about personality disorders or mental health issues? Possibly! Or did they notice and just ignore it because they were guests in our house? Possibly! Or was it because people at that time did not actively observe human behaviour? Who knows? If they had recognised a deviant characteristic, who would they have reported it to? I do know that if they had broached the topic with my mother directly, she would have just laughed it off and given them a plausible story, such were her lies. She was extremely convincing.

A doctor noticing something peculiar, could have approached my father. I think he might have listened, given that she inflicted as much abuse onto him as she did me. He might have felt having an ally would have given him some level of power to persuade his wife to get medical help. (I very much doubt it though!)

This incident that occurred around the time I was in Year 5 and had just finished working at Hoover Ltd. In Wembly. My father had probably discovered that I had been working and challenged his wife about it. Whenever she was sprung, there was always a consequence for him. It had been a Monday morning and he had gone to work. For me, it was the start of the school holidays – not a day I had looked forward to.

"Susan!" my mother had screamed. "Get in here immediately!

Here - take this axe. We are chopping up the piano. I'm sick of it lying around the house. It's old, it's in the way, and it's going!"

What my mother did that day, I will never forget. How she had stormed into my father's lounge room wielding two large and extremely heavy axes, I will never forget. The incredibly fierce and intensely angry look on her face will stay in my memory for the remainder of my life. At that moment, she was totally insane. I knew it then, and I knew there was nothing I could do to stop her. All I could do was watch in horror as she attacked my father's antique German piano.

She repeatedly yelled at me to start smashing away, but all I could do was watch her frenzy. She was obsessed, possessed, insanely angry and beyond the point of any level of control over her thoughts or actions. I remember I wasn't scared. I wasn't scared because this behaviour was so bizarre that my mind could not fully absorb and comprehend what was happening. Her anger wasn't directed at me.

I do remember wondering where the axes had come from. I knew the tools that were in the shed, and I had never seen these axes before. This leads me to believe that my mother had planned it. But… the scary part… was she able to turn on her frenzied assaults whenever she wanted to, or had something triggered this outburst that morning – if she had planned this assault, did she know it would be that morning, or was she waiting for any morning she might possibly be annoyed with my father?

I'm the pragmatist. I think the seed had been sown in her head a few days prior to the incident. She had then purchased and hidden the axes before deciding which day to attack. I think she deliberately planned for the Monday morning, when her husband would be at work, and when I was home to see her performance. I believe I was always an integral part of her actions for whatever purpose. I think she enjoyed seeing me suffer, and she certainly knew I did that morning.

My mother's aggression towards me was always fuelled by jealously. I was my father's favourite, I was smart, and I kept my emotional responses hidden from her. Whenever she taunted or attacked me, I showed her no emotion. That was how I survived all her verbal and physical assaults. That day, she wanted me to see my father's precious piano smashed to smithereens as a sign of the power that she had over him. (It also showed her total lack of any respect that she had for her husband. Like me, he was just a pawn in her power game).

And like the practical, little girl that I was, I just cleaned up. What else could I do. When she had finally finished chopping and smashing, we both took all the planks into the shed and stacked them up to be burned later, on the fire. Rubbing her hands together and laughing out loud, I had seen that all too familiar glassy look in her eye. She had been euphoric.

That night when my father returned home, I had been sitting in the scullery shelling peas. (I wasn't permitted to do any homework, so had always been given practical housework jobs to do. One night it would be peeling potatoes, another would be cleaning the pantry, another would be polishing the silver – that's how it was. Being school holidays meant no library at night).

"Oh, John, you'll never guess what a stroke of luck I had today!" she beamed at my father, as he removed his plate of steamed dinner from the stove. "A passing man called in to ask if we had any old pianos. He came in and looked at ours and gave me a great price for it. I couldn't believe it!" she screamed.

What could he say? Like me he was shell-shocked. The piano had sentimental, as well as monetary, value to him. It was a while later, when he had been doing some gardening clean up that he had discovered the wood. Some of it had been burned in the boiler, but most of it was still intact. I don't think he ever spoke to her about it. Was he afraid of her? Possibly? Was it just easier to keep the peace? Absolutely!

The night she had told my father that blatant lie, I had felt sorry for him. He had not known the lady he had married. In India, he had fallen in love with a gorgeous looking blonde lady, who had cared for him when he was sick, but who after they had married, had little care for him. All she had wanted was the middle-class status.

On returning to school after the holidays, my teacher had asked us if we had all enjoyed our time off. "You know children, as we go through life, we all experience good and bad things. We have good and bad days, but when we look back on our life, we only remember the good times."

As I lay in bed that night, I thought about this lady's words. "Is my life so different from everyone else's because when I look back at my life, I don't remember the good because the bad was so bad?"

Yes, there were brief moments of pleasure: the time I opened my bear - but then I lost him; playing dress-ups with Justine – we had been kids; the time we went on the train and boat to Belgium – I loved that; the time I ate a boiled egg and cupcake at Christine's house – I had felt special; not much else – very sad.

No-one talked about child abuse at this time. It was common practice for parents to give their children physical punishments. For me, I knew I never deserved to get whacked: punched in the head or into my ears, slapped across the face, beaten about the shoulders with a stick or hit with this same stick across my legs and arms. I wasn't being hit because I was being punished – punishment was applied to another part of the body! She didn't hit me there. Even when I was quite young, I knew there was a difference.

Physical abuse for me has never really, been an issue. When she hit me, I knew it was a definite action that left a mark. My mother knew she couldn't leave too heavy a mark, hence the blanket beating, because of the possibility of someone asking questions. She always chose the times when I wouldn't be going anywhere for a while (evenings, night-time or holidays).

The sexual abuse was something I didn't understand. She wasn't the perpetrator directly, she was the orchestrator. At eleven years of age, I had been raped, and sexually assaulted in other ways, more than forty times – and more was to come. Looking back at the total number of such assaults, after I had left home, I wondered about the conversations my mother must have had with each individual offender, that had led to each of them thinking they could do what they did. I know with Mr Roundtree, he couldn't believe his luck. Not only had my mother not reported him to the police after he had raped my sister, but she had then deliberately sent in her other child for the same treatment and more – so much more. (I cannot divulge what this man did because – readers - you would be too severely affected emotionally). An afternoon session lasted three hours – three hours of sexual activity, every week for four months. What had I done to deserve that?

Before I talk specifically about emotional abuse, an area of abuse that certainly impacted on my emotional state, was – that of neglect. When children are not provided for (clothes, food, essential items) it significantly affects their health and well-being.

Clothes:

My mother would never buy any clothing item in a shop. I was never permitted to own anything that was bought new from a shop. She gladly accepted hand-me-downs from her sister, but this didn't happen very often. There were trips to the charity shops and jumble sales, but the items she mostly purchased, or attempted to steal, were materials to make the garments I had to wear. The curtain outfits lasted until I was about eight, and then she made me a trouser suit from off-cuts she got cheaply. It was hideous and I was so ashamed to leave the house.

When walking with a group of students from my school one day, Gillian, one of my friends, had laughed, "I told my mum I had nothing to wear. She said I had plenty, but I insisted I had nothing to wear to a party. So, she bought me a lovely new dress, cardigan and shoes." Then Gillian looked devilishly at us, "But, of course I knew I really had plenty of clothes!" she laughed again.

I looked down at my poorly made trouser suit and thought, "You know what, I have nothing to wear – no, seriously – I have nothing to wear!"

This is one of the reasons now, as an adult, I choose my clothes carefully, only buying exactly the most perfect items I need. I have the most perfect pair of jeans, the most versatile pairs of leggings and the best sweaters. I love my clothes and take great pride in wearing each, and every item.

Shoes and Socks:

The first pair of new shoes I ever owned were my school shoes in Year 6. My father's sister had visited us and selected them for me. My mother had never known about them, and I had never worn them to or from the house. I had always changed into them and out of them before she saw me.

Most of the socks I wore were ones my father did not want any more. He had small feet and so his used ones were perfect for me. My plimsolls had been charity shop ones that fortunately had lasted a long time. When they became too small, I cut holes in the toes. (So funny looking back – I was very enterprising!)

Food:

By the time I was in Year 6, I had established a routine of food that I could live with. I never ate breakfast because I couldn't stomach the mouldy bread and dripping at that time in the day. There was never any juice or fruit, even though most of these primary years, my mother still collected free juice, milk and fresh fruits and vegetables from the council. I would walk up with her and ask for her week's supply. These items were for children, not adults, but there was no way my mother would have wasted any of them on either of my sisters or me.

Once at school, we were forced to drink the warm milk provided to all children each morning. By eleven a.m. I was hungry, and so drank it gratefully, even though I detested the taste, and now cannot drink anything with milk in it. Lunchtime was school dinners. These were great. Most of the other children complained about eating them, but for me, they were a hot meal that had a dessert. I knew there was nothing else much at home.

After school I always went to the library. In planning for this, I would take two of my mother's rock cakes and eat one whilst walking up to the library. I would also take a tea bag. In the library there was a hot water urn for people to make tea, which cost a penny a cup. I only needed the water, as I have always only drunk my tea without milk. On reaching the library, I would make my tea and sit in the kitchen there to dunk my second rock cake into. Then I was ready to study. Looking back at this time, I was actually happy. I was in control of my life, and I knew I could cope, which meant I could relax my nerves a little.

Weekend food was different. My father was home more and demanded we had a cooked lunch at midday and sandwiches around five p.m. So, all good – food sorted! As long as I was home for these mealtimes, no-one asked questions about how I spent my time.

Essential Items:

Here I hit a snag. My sister Justine had the same problem, except by the time I was in Year 6, she had a part-time job and could buy her own stockings, bras, underwear and sanitary protection.

I remember her having a fierce argument with my mother about wearing stockings. Justine had lost the argument, which made it equally hard for me to win, when my time came. Sanitary protection was the most repulsive argument I can remember. My mother saw no reason for me not to wash my pad out every time I used it. I was used to washing out my underwear and putting it back on soaking wet, but I wasn't doing it with this flimsy piece of material she had given me to do this job, which, do the job - it did not!

The only reason I began washing my knickers, was because my mother didn't – she saw no reason for me not to wear my pair for a week! Even to this day, I am fastidious about my underwear. It was also humiliating at school, at times when I had to change into sports clothes. How was I supposed to hide my repulsive under garments?

Enough on this topic!

How children look affects the way they behave. My lack of proper care and clothing seriously affected the way I behaved. I led a juxta positional life. At school I was well-liked and well-respected. At home, I was anything but that.

The first time my school gave out Merit Certificates, was when I was in Year 6. I received my first one about half-way through the year for being a 'Super Teacher.' My teacher had asked me to teach my sister's class English every Wednesday afternoon for an hour. I enjoyed this, and Christine never told my mother. I did lessons with this class for most of this year. Their class teacher did not even remain in the room – it was as if I were the class teacher. When my mother found the Merit Certificate, she went crazy and ripped it up. I knew that I could never bring home any more of these awards.

I also knew this would be a trigger for more time off school. And I was right!

On Wednesdays, I refused to let her keep me home, as I loved the teaching. I was a natural, born teacher – I've always known this. My teachers at school certainly recognised my ability, as they did in later years too when I was asked to teach French and English in high school.

On other days, my mother would play her tricks again. She knew she couldn't just tell me to go into the spare bedroom and go to bed for the day, because I simply would not have complied, so she started slipping something into my morning tea, which made me instantly ill. I didn't realise at first, but when I did, I instantly stopped drinking my morning cup of tea. I also became acutely aware of eating anything that she had made, such as the rock cakes.

I was now approaching the middle of Year 6 and my school began preparing us for high school. In England in 1962, all students who attended state schools were required to sit the 11+. This examination, which was a form of I.Q. (Intelligence Quotient) test that established every student's academic pathway into high school. If you passed the test, then you were allocated the closest grammar school to your address. If you failed the test, you were sent to the local secondary school. Depending on your results, you were then allocated the type of class and level of course work appropriate to your ability. Once placed in a class, there was little capacity to change levels at any time in the future.

One test – one test that has nothing to do with any curriculum work students have learned during their seven years of primary schooling, determines who will be permitted the university pathway or who will likely be a technical college candidate in the future.

As a practicing teacher now, I find this assessment practice to be archaic and irrelevant, and it really shows a complete lack of understanding of academic ability. There are people who profess that students cannot learn how to do these types of assessments, and so cannot change their I.Q. I disagree with this. Learning how to do these types of tests is similar to learning how to do cryptic crossword puzzles, once you work out the skill and then the strategy, you can learn how to do each skill type. It also helps to practise the skills, as this familiarises you with the different ways these skills are presented. A student, who has never been exposed to these types of tests before, is unlikely to do well, but a student who has had extensive practice, even if not particularly academically clever, can score well. I have proven this many times in my teaching of students in my current life who are required to sit these types of tests for Selective School placements.

The day of the 11+ arrives. I had not slept well, worrying about how well I will do in this assessment. I still had my secret dreams and plans to be a teacher, despite my mother's insistence I train for nursing. (I think she always knew I was never going to be a nurse – she knew I had my heart set on teaching!)

I'm sitting at the breakfast table drinking tea (I had made).

"Susie, good luck with your tests today. I'll be thinking of you," my father smiles as he leaves for work.

The door closes.

"Don't think you're going to go to school today!" my mother immediately yells at me. "I have other plans for you!"

My heart sank. How I desperately wanted to go to Harrow Grammar School. I knew I was smart enough to get in, but now this doorway would be closed to me. What could I do?

"Come on, hurry up, we have work to do."

That day she took me on her district rounds. I blanket bathed old ladies, made them cups of tea, cleaned their houses, helped them with their toileting, took their dogs for walks, cooked their lunches and did jig-saw puzzles with them. My mother's patients liked me. They called me, 'Sister's daughter.' The doctors liked me too. In those days, these elderly folk had doctors who made regular house visits, especially if the district nurse was involved in their daily care and medication treatments. Only one of these doctors asked me why I wasn't at school. His son was in my class.

I had looked at him, and not answered verbally – only non-verbally!

My father had been furious, when he had found out, but what could he do? I had missed out on my chance of an academic pathway in high school and so must accept the situation. As it turned out my father accepted a promotion's job shortly after this episode, which meant that our family would be moving to Cardiff at the end of the year. (This move did not change my academic status, though. I still would not be able to access a grammar school in Wales).

I was bitterly disappointed.

At that point in time in my life, I hated my mother. I knew that so much of her treatment of me impacted on me as emotional abuse. She bullied me, belittled me, made me wear clothes that looked awful, cut my hair so that I looked awful, criticised me openly to people she met – I was never good enough for her. She saw no good in me at all. I was just her slave – someone to punch, prod and poke whenever she felt like making me cry.

I never cried in front of her, though. The hardest aspect of emotional abuse is defining it as a single act that can be packaged in some concrete form. If I had told anyone about how I was being treated, they would have laughed at me – no-one would have believed me, and so I always knew I had to keep my problems to myself.

So, what do the medics say about emotional abuse?
- *yelling at the person*
- *name-calling*
- *making insults to deliberately hurt them emotionally*
- *attempting to make a person question their own sanity*
- *invading privacy*
- *giving punishments that are not deserved*

- *trying to control a person's life*
- *isolating someone from family and friends*
- *making subtle or overt threats*

Some advice that they give:
1. If you think you're being emotionally abused, don't blame yourself – it's not your fault.
2. There are no right or wrong ways to feel about the way you've been abused.
3. Emotional abuse is not a normal behaviour, but your feelings are.

What have been some of my mother's abusive behaviours towards me?

- Yelling and screaming at me daily.
- Calling me stupid, useless and worthless.
- Hauling me physically in front of a mirror and saying I'm fat and ugly, and that no-one will like me.
- Insulting me in front of other people to deliberately exert power over me.
- Neglecting to provide my daily needs – force feeding me to make me ill.
- Leaving me to die when I was very sick as a small child.
- Imprisoning me in a room for eight months.
- Giving me drugs to make me sleep or make me ill.
- Invading my privacy.
- Deliberately allowing me to be raped and sexually assaulted in horrible ways.
- Denying me access to a continued education and instead making me go out to work.
- Making threats at me.

- Attacking me physically for being good or doing well at something.
- Hauling me out into the snow or rain to clean outside wearing inadequate clothing and footwear, and at three a.m.
- Making me do extremely difficult physical tasks impossible for a small child to do.

What do the medics say about the short-term and long-term effects of emotional abuse?

They say it is normal to feel a level of:

1. Short-Term
- *confusion*
- *fear*
- *hopelessness*
- *shame*

Yes - all the above. At twelve years of age, I had felt these emotions daily for ten years. (That is not exactly short-term.)

2. Long-Term

They say emotionally abused children may develop:
- *anxiety*
- *chronic pain*
- *guilt*
- *insomnia*
- *social withdrawal or loneliness*

No, none of these because I refused to allow myself to be so severely affected by my mother's taunts. I learned how to wear a suit of armour.

What do the medics say about children's abuse going unrecognised?

They say that a child might:
- *become socially withdrawn*
- *suffer sleep disorders*

- *experience regression*
- *develop eating disorders*
- *have prolonged headaches*
- *develop heart disease*
- *develop mental health issues*
- *develop obesity or engage in substance abuse*

Yes, some of these. I certainly became socially withdrawn and lacked confidence, self-esteem and a good self-concept.

Sleep disorders: as a child I lived in fear that my mother would come into my room at any time during the night to haul me out of bed for some reason. I was also fearful she would find me using my fingers to block out the sounds of the house – I would push my fingers into both ears to hide myself away inside myself. I never slept well during my time at home, and I still don't as an adult.

Regression: I slipped back academically during my teenage years because of the severe tornado effect on my nerves. They were strung so tight, many of them snapped, leaving me with an undiagnosed and untreated nervous breakdown.

Eating Disorders: anorexia nervosa and bulimia for an extensive part of my life after leaving home at the age of eighteen.

Mental Health Issues: I say, yes, but those who know me say, no. Interestingly, after I had moved away from home, I shared a house with three other teachers. A boyfriend of mine was at the house one day and made this comment:

"All these people you live with are 'nuts!' You're the sanest one here!"

I had smiled – that was such a compliment!

This next section of my story is the high school era.

Those first ten years of my life I survived by planning every day carefully. There were always the unguarded moments, and these I knew I just had to ride, like being in the wind of a very violent storm. I forced myself to hang on.

The New Day

As I run at break of dawn,
The only sounds are the songbirds' call.
This lonely hour redeems them all,
The new day dawns once more.
As life begins the sunshine looms
A brilliant red entwined with blue.
Cascading beams of light illume
The day's fantastic hues.
I keep on running into day,
As sunlight shines to show the way.
My body warmed by morning rays –
Fresh energy displays.
The running helps my mind unwind,
Releasing strife of every kind.
Refreshing thoughts invade my mind –
A freedom rare to find.
With rising heat my body aches,
With every muscle wide awake,
The day begins and though I shake,
I know I'll never break.

True freedom is running at daybreak.

Moving House

Moving from primary school, my family also moved house. I'd survived these difficult childhood years, but would I survive my teen ones? My biggest challenge was not knowing what was around the corner each day, as well as some level of not being in control of how I chose to spend my time. Ever since the age of four, I had walked the streets alone, but even though I planned my days carefully, there was always the unknown.

"Susan, you're to go shopping to buy these items.

Susan, you're to spend the day with my patients.

Susan, go next door and clean their house.

Susan, I've organised for you to look after a child for the day in their house."

And so on… and so on…

I never minded if the tasks I was given were outside the house. If they were home tasks, then I found the day extremely difficult to cope with. My mother got on my nerves. I couldn't stand her cigarette smoking or her smoker's cough. I couldn't stand the little ticking noises she made that made me cringe. I wished I could lose all my senses, so that I wouldn't have to see, hear, smell or touch her.

Moving house was a huge imposition on my time. My mother never did any housework and neither did my sisters. When my father received his promotion, she had been irate that it meant moving to another place. The only positive thing for her, was that his salary increased enough for her not to have to work again. This was an incentive that she liked. She liked being at home, and if it meant her husband would give her housekeeping money each week, then she would gladly stay home.

Another incentive she had was the visit from the gypsies.

I was always confused why my mother agreed to move from Harrow to Cardiff.

She was a Lancashire lass, used to the country life in these mid to northland parts. She loved living in London, almost as if this epitomised everything that was middle-class as opposed to her working-class roots. For many people in England at this time, one's socio-economic status was very important. Coming from a working-class background it was expected that girls would become diligent housewives and marry labourers or tradesmen. In retrospect I think my mother would have been more suited to a practical, working-class lad, rather than a middle-class, educated businessman whose only hobbies were watching cricket, reading literary novels and listening to classical music – none of which she shared.

She detested everything about my father's interests and lifestyle. As a couple, they never spent time together, either at home or going out. They never gave each other birthday or Christmas gifts, and they never mentioned their wedding anniversary during the time I lived in their house. Once I had moved away, my father had a function for their fiftieth.

So, selling up and moving to Wales, wow! That had come out of the blue!

So, what was in it for my mother? There had to be something more than giving up her job. She loved her job – I found it hard to believe she was seriously agreeing to this. (No, there were plans!)

My father too had made his plans. He was excited. This job

was a senior accountant with British Rail's new Sealink service across the English Channel. In his work in London, he was well respected, as he also became in Cardiff. He and his wife were afforded the luxury of free First-Class travel anywhere in Europe. Once the Sealink service was operational, he enjoyed travelling to France for the day to buy wine, and to enjoy a nice meal aboard the luxury ferry. My mother, of course, never went with him.

"Suzels, it's going to be such fun in Cardiff. There's a castle in the main street, and a beautiful park where we can go for walks. We have a house picked out, and our lives will be different, I promise you."

My mother had simply scowled at him, on hearing his words.

The next day…

"John. You'll never guess who came to the house today! Quite out of the blue – a family of gypsies. You'll never guess what they told me!"

My father wasn't interested, but as his wife rarely spoke to him as he ate his evening meal, he listened to what she had to say.

"They told me we were moving, but that we'd be back within the year. Oh, John, I was so relieved to hear this. Now I can go to Cardiff and know I'll be back before I know it. John, in thinking about this house, I'm thinking we don't sell it. I'm thinking we develop it into flats – one up and one down. This house will be perfect."

So, that was her plan!

"Jess, that would mean getting a loan for our Cardiff house, as well as paying for the renovations. We simply can't afford that," he had looked directly at her.

Sitting at the table, as I was that night, I could feel the tension in my father's voice. He always knew he could never win a fight with his wife, and he knew he wasn't going to win this one. If she had set her sights on this project, then he was never going to change her mind.

Of course, my mother was never going to move to Cardiff – not long-term. She now had a plan. Over the next six months or so she would live in the Harrow house while the renovations were made, and then by the time the flats would be ready for letting, she could put the second layer of her plan into place – to carry out the gypsies' prophecy of returning to Harrow.

"Jess how are we going to fund this renovation?" my father had looked at his wife anxiously.

"Oh, John, I've got some money put away. I'll pay for this."

Sitting there, as I did that day, this news was good news for me because it meant I would see less of my mother over the next eight to ten months. With a project to get her teeth into, I hoped she was less likely to get her claws into me! But…

She lied about the savings. I found out what her plans were.

When her father had passed away, he had left my sisters and myself two thousand pounds each. The money had been placed in a trust fund for us to receive when we turned twenty-one. Justine, at this time, was fifteen years old, and so my mother had plenty of time before Justine would be entitled to her inheritance. The renovations were priced at exactly six thousand pounds. When the bank manager had refused her a loan for this work, she had taken this money as hers. (She never paid it back!)

The move went well. Now with a project to manage, and the funds to pay for it, my mother set about packing up our house as quickly as she could. She was keen to get us out.

I loved Cardiff. The house my parents bought was only three years old and in a nice, new part of the town. It was such a change from the dirty, rat-infested alleyway our old house had been next to. There were three bedrooms, a large living area and a nice, modern kitchen. The back garden was spacious and great for playing cricket, which we did with my father at the weekends. Yes, life was looking up.

I liked my school. My father had bought me their uniform. Wow! For the first time in my life, I was wearing what every other girl at the school was wearing. The uniform code was strict, and I had no problem with that. I wore my uniform – including the beret, with pride. On the first day at the school, I had noticed the principal watching me. (I knew that he had sensed something different about me. I now realise he was seeing my 'V' sign on my forehead).

As I hadn't sat the 11+, I could not access the grammar stream in the school. Instead, I was placed in 7A, and I was happy with this. My English teacher was a Mr Taylor, who I discovered was the famous actress, Elizabeth Taylor's brother. He looked like her, and I felt honoured to know him. He liked me, and so I did well in English.

With my mother not around much in the first part of the school year, I was much happier and excelled in school. I learned to speak French and came first in the class in the Christmas exams. Interestingly, I came fourth in Welsh. Interestingly because many of the students were from Welsh speaking backgrounds! I also came first in most other subjects. It was a good school, and I was motivated to do my best. With no distractors and less stress, I was able to do my homework at home and enjoy going out with friends. Hey, life was becoming normal!

At Christmas time the lake at the bottom of our road, iced over, and my friends and I would go ice-skating. I loved it. I loved going for walks, bike rides and adventures in the castle. It was a time when I felt so much better about myself and was beginning to build my confidence and sense of self-esteem.

However, it was all short-lived and soon to change.

We had moved to Cardiff for the start of the new school year in September, and renovations had commenced immediately. By the following March, both flatlets were completed with full occupancy. My mother had enjoyed overseeing her project, travelling to Harrow every Monday morning and returning to Cardiff on Friday afternoons. Once the tenants had signed their leases, my mother could no longer stay in the house, but would still travel up once a month to collect rents.

She enjoyed travelling by herself. Like her husband, she was afforded First-Class free travel, including meal services. Travelling around the English countryside in autumn is very pleasant, but as winter progressed, she had to curtail her travel plans.

As soon as the warmer spring weather returned, so did her sojourns.

She hated her weekends in Cardiff and couldn't wait for Mondays. Having to spend the winter with her family, made her ill at ease, and I knew to avoid her at these times. Most weekends I would spend time with my friends and arrive home late and go straight to bed. My mother didn't bother me much over this winter period, I think because she was too involved in working out her plan.

She knew she couldn't stay permanently in Wales. It was not where she wanted to be. She had no job, no friends and nowhere to go. Once she began travelling again, her monthly travel routine was not enough for her. That's when I knew she was hatching her scheme. Part of this scheme, I think, was getting back some of the control she had over me, that over the past six months or so, she had lost. And so, once more, her plays and ploys started.

It had been a Sunday afternoon, when she had first attacked me. I was just about to go out with one of my girlfriends when…

"Susan, come her," my mother had screamed.

I instantly obeyed.

As I approached her space, she grabbed me by my hair and hauled me in front of a large, stand-up mirror.

"Look at you, girl!" she screamed again at me, clutching me so tightly I could scarcely move. "You are so fat and ugly, just like you were when you were little. It's about time I cut your hair to make you look more respectable."

During these past few months, with my mother in London, my hair had grown quite long. I had been in the habit of trimming the ends and my fringe myself, and I liked the length and look of my hair. Yanking me down on a stool, she began to slice my hair off. There was no point in me struggling, as she was far too fierce and much too strong. I knew I just had to grin and bear it. When she had finished, I was beside myself with anger, hurt, shame and humiliation. I couldn't look at myself in the mirror. My friend would be here any minute – what could I do?

Just then there was a knock at the door. My mother opened it. I was standing in the hallway, tears streaming down my face, unable to do or say anything. I felt so ashamed and so ugly. (That occasion was one of the rare times she did see me cry. I couldn't help it – I was so upset).

My friend was lovely. "Why don't we go for a walk?" she smiled at me.

I nodded and we left to go and sit in the park. It was cold in the early evening air, but we huddled together and talked. She made me feel better about myself, but I knew I couldn't go to school looking like I did. When I returned home, I stormed into my father's room and stood facing him, "You never went to work for a week when she cut your hair. How can I go to school looking like this? If she ever cuts my hair again – I'll kill her!" I yelled at him and then left the room.

The next day I walked around Cardiff until it was home time. My mother had not known I'd taken the day off school. When I returned home, I acted as if I'd had a normal, busy day, and then set about preparing the evening meal. During the time that my mother had been absent during the weekdays, I had become accustomed to cooking dinner for my sisters and father.

My father had given me housekeeping and loved that we shared an evening meal. With my mother now joining us, she hated that I enjoyed this cooking time. (I think this was the catalyst for why she thought I wanted to be a Home Science teacher. When I was sixteen, we had both argued vehemently about this – I had never thought this was my teaching pathway. In my sights I was always going to be a teacher of French, but she never knew this). As a child she had never let me cook anything, again I think because she knew I was good at it. No, the kitchen was always her private realm.

Sitting eating dinner as we did that night, I sensed my mother's annoyance. She had never been a good cook, and she had never had any incentive to cook a nice meal for her family. I felt her jealousy. She sensed the closeness of the relationship I had developed with my father, and she was insanely jealous. To sit at the dinner table eating a meal I had cooked, listening to my father's compliments, sent her brain into a frenzy. There was no way she was going to allow me to cook our dinner every night! And there was no way she was going to allow him to give me money to do it!

"John, I think we'll go back to afternoon tea instead of

dinner, now that I'm home again."

Afternoon tea meant anything left over from Sunday lunch that was edible. My father was disappointed, but for him, he still had dinner – we didn't. What was worse too, was that school dinners had ceased, and so there was precious little for me to eat during the day. After I had washed up that night, I once again confronted my father. "If we are not having dinner at night any more, you need to give me lunch money."

He had looked up at me and quietly said, "Susie, I have something for you." He then reached into his work bag and pulled out a brown paper bag. My secretary bought this for you. I opened it and cried. She had bought me a wig. It was lovely. It was similar to my hairstyle and colour before my mother had hacked away. I was so touched that my father's secretary had gone to so much trouble to match a wig especially for me.

"Oh, thank you. It's lovely. I'll need a sick note too," I smiled at him.

I never told my mother about the wig, but like the situation with the force feeding – having a fall-back plan meant I never had to worry about that behaviour again. I would always have my wig!

So, how did my mother coerce my father into returning to London? She couldn't – she didn't, not at that time. She knew she had to keep her plan furtive until it was time to strike. The next time she attacked was a Sunday night. "John, I'm taking Susan to London tomorrow to get her teeth done."

All I could think, was, "She just wants an excuse to go to London."

She had always used my teeth as an excuse to bully me. When I was in Kindergarten, at five years of age, she made me walk from my school every Monday night to the dentist in downtown Harrow. It was a forty-five-minute walk for me. My appointment time would be six o'clock, but I would get there around 4.45 p.m. I would patiently wait in the waiting room until I saw the dentist. No-one ever came with me, not even when I had gas to have teeth removed, or fillings done without injections. I went every week for over two months – what treatments had she organised for me to have done? (What mother does that to her child?)

On one occasion, the dentist was very busy. I had sat there until seven p.m. No-one came up to me or asked me if I was all right. Eventually, I became so frightened that I went to the reception to ask if anyone was going to see me. Almost in tears, I had looked at the lady, who had said it wouldn't be much longer. (I think they had just forgotten about me!)

So, now I'm off to the dentist again. "Why?" I ask myself.

Once in London, my mother had arranged for me to see an orthodontist, who recommended I have braces fitted. (So, that's my mother's ploy. I'll need to go often!)

Once my dental appointments were scheduled, we returned home later that day. Having sorted out times for us to return to London on a regular basis, my mother set about putting in place the next part of her plan. (I knew it was all part of a scheme – it was just hard to work out just what she had in mind. How could I know – her mind was so warped!)

Ah, but then it happened!

The weather around Easter time was becoming sunny in the afternoons. My mother bought a budgie. In the cage she placed a little mirror that sparkled in the sunlight. When it sparkled, it caught the sun's rays reflecting onto the front room curtains. Being the Easter school holidays, my days were once more filled with chores that took me out of the house.

It was the Tuesday afternoon of the first week at exactly two thirty p.m. when the fire started. My mother had whizzed off to buy her cigarettes, and I was returning from buying her the items she needed from the supermarket. Shopping in this neighbourhood was so much easier than Harrow because the shops were closer, and there was a supermarket.

As I approached the house, I could see smoke coming from the lounge room windows. Leaving the shopping bags on the ground I tore into the house to find the curtains ablaze. I quickly ripped them down from their railings and smothered them like I had done my grandmother's bedding all those years ago. I think my mother would have liked the fire to have been more progressed than it was. Once again, I had thwarted her plan. Even so, it was enough to convince my father to consider moving back to Harrow. I think he knew that his wife was desperately unhappy, and he feared what else she might do. There was nothing else he could do, except put in for a transfer back to his old job in London. He had been bitterly disappointed.

My mother, however, was anything but disappointed. She was in her element! Her plan had worked, she was house-hunting in Harrow – thank you gypsies! And so it was that we moved back.

Opportunity Knocks

When opportunity knocks
You answer the door,
For you just never know
When he'll make his encore.
Your chances are seldom –
A rare calling card,
So, take every moment
And listen so hard.
You'll hear all the sounds
That beckon your way,
But don't lose a second
Along life's highway.
Be watchful for dangers
That often lurk deep.
They'll hinder your chances
If you don't take that leap.

Throughout my childhood, my most effective strategy was walking for hours. This always helped me calm down and unwind my nerves. As an adult, I enjoy running for fun. For years I have run fifteen kilometres each day, followed by a three-kilometre swim before trekking off to work.

The 'C' Word

The title of this story will reveal its message in due course.

Without so much as a day to wait until the dust settled, my mother decided on a house in North Harrow. The house needed work, which gave her the opportunity to move immediately and begin wallpapering and painting. I was happy to see her go. The rest of us remained in Cardiff until our house was sold. There was still one term to go before the end of the school year, and it gave me a chance to do well in the end of year exams – and to let my hair grow!

My story is a story that must be told. I knew, growing up, that other children had bad home lives. I was aware that some children were physically or sexually abused by their parents in ways that I wasn't. I felt for those children as I feel for that little girl, who was me. She never did anything wrong and did not deserve the life she was forced to endure. Parents are supposed to love and protect their children. How many children can say they have never used the word 'Mum' when referring to their mother? How many children can say that they hate their mother so much, that they want to take a large carving knife to her, and stab her until she bleeds out? By the time I was thirteen, I was so angry about the things that she had done to me, that I just wanted to kill her.

Having this respite of time from May to September in 1963 was Heaven. If I'd known what was around the corner, however, I think I would have ended my life.

In thinking about the kind of mother that I was, my one goal for my children was to provide them with a happy home life. It was important to me that both my children went to bed each night – happy. Whatever conflicts arose during the day, it was always important to me that any issues were resolved before bedtime. My son had hated me one day, when my husband had asked me to make a meat pie for his dinner. This meant my children would also have this dish. My son had taken one look at the pie and scowled, "I'm not eating pie for dinner!"

I had immediately removed his plate and said, "Then that's dinner for you! Goodnight."

Looking at me aghast, and sneering at me, he had obeyed and gone to do his homework. An hour later he had come to me and said, "Mum, I ate the pie. Thank you."

"Of course, you did," I said to myself. I'm a behaviouralist. Too often today, though, I hear children say to their parents:

"I don't want that ham sandwich. It's too boring. Get me something else."

"I don't want to eat the potato because it's touching the carrots."

'Wh, wh, what!" I think to myself. "Really?"

In my job as a teacher, I would frequently take students on school camp. The first night most of them would comment on the food and leave large amounts, but on the second night they would eat everything. Yes, if they are hungry, they will eat what they are given.

I would have eaten any dinner I was given! (Well, almost – not the raw liver!)

I was grateful for anything that resembled food! Most of my life to this point, the only decent food I'd received was school dinners. My mother always cooked cabbage, potatoes and liver on Saturdays, and a roast lamb on Sundays. Any left-over food was then placed in the larder to be eaten by my mother for her lunches each day. We got to eat the dripping from the lamb with bread and marmite. By Wednesday, the bread was always dry and going mouldy. I got used to eating this and accepted that this was what I got.

The liver on Saturdays for me, though, was raw.

"Susan, the doctor has said you need iron. He has said you either eat two slices of raw liver each week or a bar of Cadbury Bourneville chocolate. Well, I'm not buying you the chocolate, so you'll eat the liver."

I couldn't. I tried. I cried.

"Jess don't force her," my father had interjected.

So, each Saturday after that I would only eat the potatoes and cabbage. I was happy with that. On Sundays my mother was equally happy I didn't eat the roast meat, because that meant more for her. For dessert she always made herself a milky bread and butter pudding. I knew she had used the mouldy bread, and so would always decline to eat this.

Likewise, the milk always smelled 'off' – even to this day I cannot watch someone drink a glass of milk or eat bread and butter pudding!

Now, chocolate cake! That would have been something I would have wanted!

Yes, when I think back to the life my mother made me lead, it is no wonder I become so jealous of girls who have lovely mums. I really wish I'd had a mum who had loved and cared for me.

In September 1963, my sisters, myself and my father travelled by train back to Harrow. My mother had returned to Cardiff after we had packed everything, and then travelled with the truck to the new house. Anytime I spent away from my mother was time to treasure. I coveted that time. I was so grateful for the time to relax. Relaxing when my mother was in the house, was not something anyone could do – at any time the atmosphere could be cut with a knife.

The new year at school started. Finishing up the year in Cardiff, the principal had come to me and said, "Sue, I'm so disappointed you are not continuing to Year 8 here, because you would have been an excellent candidate to sit the 12+ and then join the academic class in the school here. (I had come first in almost all my subjects, as I had done in the first exams). Not being able to sit this 12+ disappointed me, but I had to accept it.

So, fronting up to the principal of the local secondary school in Harrow, the principal had said, "Susan, your sister was in the 'B' stream of this school and so that's where I'm placing you."

Another new student had also enrolled that day. Her name was Jane, and when she was placed in the 'A' stream, I looked at Mrs Wall, the principal, and said, "But, you've put Jane in the top class. Why can't I go into this class too?"

"Jane gave me her school report. Bring me yours tomorrow and I'll decide then."

So, the next day I fronted up to her office with my school report.

"Yes, you can go into 8A, but…"

The lady had looked oddly at me and then smiled, "If you don't come first in every subject, I'll put you back in 8B."

At the end of the term, I came top in every subject. I scored 100% in French. The teacher was Mrs Wall. She came up to me in class, after she had given out the results, and said, "I want you to teach your class French from now onwards. I'm also giving you a class in Year 7 to teach for English.

And so it was that I started teaching English and French in the school.

Coming top in every subject did not do me any favours, though. As it turned out, Jane had come second in every subject – so my classmates were not very happy with either of us! I had no friends in the school at this time. I would lift my desk lid and read unkind notes left by rankled students. Once I started teaching the class, however, things changed – they viewed and treated me differently. My lessons were more practical and interesting than Mrs Wall's had been, and I gradually formed some friendships.

Back at home, now in our new house, my mother became annoyed when she discovered I was doing well at school. On reading my school report, she had become irritate. My father, however, had been so proud. Whenever he gloated to their friends, my mother would scowl and find something to criticise me for. I learned to ignore these remarks. There's a term for this type of strategy. It's called 'grey rocking.'

One becomes a grey rock. A large grey boulder is untouchable. It is solid and impervious. It is difficult to budge and gives off no emotion whatsoever. It has no face and so cannot look anyone in the eye, instead preferring to focus on the ground that grounds it. I learned to become this grey rock. The more I was kicked around, the more resilient I became, covering my external surface with layers of debris that strengthened and protected my fragile internal self. Emotional abuse leaves you with a very fragile sense of self. I wrote this verse many eons ago:

Tears on the outside fall to the ground and are gently washed away.

Tears on the inside fall on the soul and stay... and stay...

and stay…

When people knock our external frame, we don't remember the pain. It goes away after a while. When people knock our internal frame, we do not forget. We cannot forget. Everyday we squeeze out the emotion that builds and must be released. Even to this day, there is never a day that goes by, when I don't feel the need to squeeze out the built-up tension from these past memories.

The grey rock protects the mind, and in my case, it needed to, as at thirteen years of age, my mind was as frangible as it was ever likely to get. I could survive the school days, but not the home days. I never knew what my mother's next ploy would be. The more I succeeded at school, the more she plotted to destroy me emotionally.

It was just after receiving my first end-of-term report at Christmas 1963, that she deployed her next ploy. There was still a week of school before the Christmas break. My mother was sewing in the front lounge room, as I entered the door. Arriving home from school each day, the first thing I always did was make myself a cup of coffee. I liked my coffee strong and black, with a little sugar.

Going upstairs to my bedroom, I sensed something was not right.

Looking across at my bed, I couldn't see the school books I had left there that morning. I shared a room with my younger sister and between the two beds, there was little space for anything else. The wardrobe and all the cupboards were filled with my mother's tins and packets of food. The only work space I had was my bed.

"I don't suppose you know where all my school books are?" I opened the lounge room door to ask her.

"No, haven't seen them," she looked me full in the face, not blinking an eye lid.

"Well, someone must have moved them, because they are not there," I said quite firmly this time.

"Well, I don't know where they are," she didn't even look up this time, but kept on sewing as if she hadn't a care in the world.

Just as I was about to leave and close the door behind me, she spoke in a very quiet voice, "You'll be sorry when I'm gone."

I froze. "What does she mean by that?" I asked myself. Walking back into the room and facing her, I said, "What do you mean by that?"

I had her attention: she wanted me to be worried: I was worried. Looking up at me, her face was as still and as emotionless as a grey rock without a face. "You'll be sorry when I'm gone, " she repeated her words. "The doctor has given me a year. You'll be sorry this time next year!"

I could get no more out of her that night. "Is she playing some kind of game with me, or is she really sick?" I asked myself as I returned upstairs. She certainly wanted me to think that she was really sick. "I know she has done something to my books. Is this the reason she is trying to cover up now with this health ploy?"

My father was home late that night, and so I couldn't ask him until the next day. He was as surprised as I was, when I confronted him.

"So, it's a ploy!" I smirk to myself. "Well, where are my books?"

Looking in the garbage bin, I find my books – all ripped up and left scattered in the bottom of the bin. She hadn't even tried to conceal her act. She had been so angry I'd done well at school, that she had destroyed all my work!

"Did she now deserve the 'C' word though? No, not even I would wish this for her.

To be continued…

Be True to Self

Whatever path we take in life
We have the power to choose the way
We think is right for us.
That's not to say we're always right.
We often make mistakes
Without us knowing why.
We have been given many gifts –
The power of thought and word and deed.
The best, of course, is love.
When things don't always go as planned
We often look to lay our blame
On others, as it's easier
To ease our grieving hearts.
It's so much harder to be true
To self, and face all our mistakes
With courage and with strength.
But when we do we know we'll find
That happiness, that only we
Know leads to faithful love.

The 'C' Word Continued

In looking back on my childhood years, I can honestly say that there was never a time when my mother said a kind word to me, or gave me a hug or kiss, or read me a story, or even shared something nice about her day. From the time that I can remember, she had only ever viewed me as 'the enemy.' Her words to me were only ever castigatory or criticisms spat venomously at me. I found these harsh, cruelly conveyed words to be so difficult to digest and believe because at school everyone liked me and said complimentary words to me. I led a juxtaposition life. I knew that her words were lies, being used as a tool to taunt me. Even to this day I find it hard to fathom that a mother would, could, be so cruel to her child.

I know that my mother must have endured something terrible in her childhood, which resulted in her personality disorder. I didn't create any of her deviant behaviours. I know she targeted me because her marriage was not a success. When my father began showing definite signs of favouritism towards me, she became insanely jealous of these special attentions I received, which she didn't.

My mother regularly said to Justine and me that she only wanted our younger sister, Christine; that Christine was her favourite. Christine was the youngest in a family of three girls and so was my mother. Christine had flowing blond hair, as did she. Christine was to be the best, the most attractive, the most prized possession she could own. She took Christine everywhere with her and delighted in 'showing her off' to all her friends. She boasted about how wonderful Christine was at every opportunity, even when Justine and I were in the room.

"Look at this gorgeous child," my mother would say. "Christine is so clever, unlike Susan here who is so stupid. I don't know why Susan can't be more like Christine. She is such an embarrassment to me."

At these times I would be 'the grey rock.' I would sit there and look at the ground. On most occasions, when her words were very harsh, and so deliberately untrue, I knew not to argue with her, but to just leave the room. I rarely let her see me cry because I hated her knowing that she had affected me emotionally, but I also knew that leaving the room meant that she had won – I was affected.

I did once stand my ground and argue with her. The ladies who were enjoying their tea and cake had looked up and stared at me.

No-one challenged my mother!

"How dare you speak to me like that! How dare you be so insulting to me when I have my friends here!"

Her words had been spat out venomously. She had then stood up and slapped me hard across the face. "Now get out of here!"

I did.

I hadn't been rude to her. Even to this day when I am annoyed with someone, I am never rude. Yes, I told her that what she had said about me was untrue, but I had not raised my voice, or been disrespectful to her in any way.

My mother saw me as such a huge threat in her attempts to make Christine the best of all of us. No matter how hard she tried, she couldn't change my destiny, and she couldn't change what

Christine was. Christine was not academic. She never did well in school, and certainly was never a prefect or a representative of anything at school, as I was. I was Head Girl for two years, represented the school in Public Speaking for three years, was selected as the Leading Lady in all school plays, I performed in, and became a teacher at the school on a full teaching load in the senior years. No other student had ever done these things.

How my mother had hated this! How she had hated the night my father had made her accompany him to a school function, when I was giving a speech. I can still see her sitting in the school assembly room, scowling at me. She was squirming with sheer hatred and loathing for me. Walking home afterwards, she had continued to squirm having to listen to my father's congratulatory remarks. He was an excellent public speaker and was so proud I had this attribute too.

I have already mentioned the occasion when my sister Justine found my Public Speaking trophy and said, "Look what Susan won today."

My mother had grabbed the trophy and sneered, "They only gave you that because they felt sorry for you!"

Yes, that had been hurtful, because I had known it wasn't true. That day I had travelled to another school site, had been required to present several prepared and impromptu speeches, and had sat and answered questions put to me by a panel of judges. It had been a rigorous competition, and I had deservedly won. I had gone to bed that night and thought, *Why can't she just be proud of me for once?*

No, she couldn't, and I knew then that she never would – no matter how hard I tried.

After the episode with the ripped schoolbooks, I decided to let that incident pass without further fuss. I learned that this was always the best pathway out of a situation. I knew I just had to accept that my work had been destroyed and the New Year would mean new books. I would be smarter, though, this time and not leave them lying around.

In a few days it would be Christmas. These holidays were always the most difficult to get through. I had made a strong bond with a friend, Lynne, from my school. Lynne was my haven. She lived about a mile from my house and needed my friendship as much as I needed hers. I could spend every day at her house, and she would still want me to spend every night and eat every meal – so this Christmas – I did, or at least I had planned to, until…

"Susan, it's Christmas Eve and I need you to help out some of my patients, who will need cleaning done, shopping and cooking," she had waltzed into the kitchen at the exact moment she knew I was about to leave for Lynne's.

"Do these patients **not** have any family members who can help out?" I had been annoyed by this sudden change to my plans. Lynne would also be upset with me if I cancelled my day with her.

"No, they don't, which is why I've said **you** will go."

"Are you **not** going to visit them today?" I had looked quizzically at her when I saw she was not wearing her nurse's uniform.

"No, I told you, the doctor has only given me a year, and so I must rest over Christmas. **You** will have to go and see to **all** my patients who will need help over this time."

(I have deliberately bolded these words to show my annoyance at this rude interruption, not just to my plans for that day, but for the entire Christmas period, as well as to show my mother's obvious enjoyment at the level of power she wielded over me).

"Wh, what?" I looked questioningly at her. "I'm not the district nurse!"

My mother had placed me in this situation many times before. There were procedures I had been asked to do that I was not qualified to do. I was really unsure of where I stood in this whole issue of providing services to her patients. It wasn't that I minded helping out, but this was not really what she was asking me to do – I knew that and so did she! I was thirteen years old!

"But… is she really sick?" I asked myself as I headed off to her first patient.

So, let's consider this 'C' word.

I am not in the practice of using inappropriate language in my daily chit-chats with family and friends. I do, however, acknowledge that there is an appropriate place for some aspects of it in describing events portrayed in some of my stories.

There are some words I never use because they are either too vulgar, or because I can find better ones. The trick is always to insert these delicacies of text constructions in ways that are clever, suitable or serve their intended purpose. Too many people in their oral language think that it is 'smart' to use certain inappropriate words, but unless these have been specifically crafted for effect, their effect is a very 'un-classy' language choice.

I have already discussed how I use the 'f' codes in my stories. This code represents the level of anger or misappropriation I have felt towards any event.

The 'C' word in this case, however, is not what you think! Even though I have been well-aware of the existence of this word since Mr Roundtree used to use it, when I was five years old, I have never used it and nor will I.

No, the 'C' word that I am going to refer to is the word

'cancer.' Cancer has a habit of appearing unexpectedly, unwelcomingly and without manners!

After my mother had callously informed me that she had only one year left to live, I was unsure if her words were really, true, or if she were using this notion as a tool to taunt me with. My father hadn't said anything, and no-one in the house was talking about it. Over this Christmas period she had not looked sick. She had continued to smoke her cigarettes, cough up her guts every morning and cook and eat her favourite foods every day. Nothing had changed, except I was attending to her patients. It surprised me that the doctors I met with every day never asked questions. I think there were two reasons for this:

1. they had become used to seeing me in these people's homes, and

2. I was competent.

I had one question, though? Was she getting paid?

After she had completed all the redecorating of the new house in North Harrow, she had returned to her district job. She had relinquished her hospital shifts and never returned to those duties. She liked her district rounds. She liked her patients, and they liked her. She knew she was good at her job. My thoughts were that she did not want anyone knowing about her health situation at that point in time. She told me about her cancer because she needed me to cover for her over the Christmas period.

Going out every day, including the Christmas and New Year weekends, had kept me busy and away from my mother. It had been one way to survive, and I wasn't unhappy helping out in this way.

When it came time to return to school, I was curious as to what her plans were. Was she returning to work, and if not, who was going to look after her patients now?

It had been the night before the school term started, when I had overheard my mother discussing her job with someone on the phone.

Oh, so that was it? She had me cover for her until this new lady could start after Christmas. That meant she got paid!

Wow! I had thought. *How devious, but how scary for me because that meant she really was sick.*

It wasn't long after the start of the New Year in 1964 that my mother began to show signs of being unwell. The first time I noticed her condition, was on returning home from school and finding her asleep on the lawn in the garden. Going into the kitchen to make my coffee, as I always did, I hadn't noticed her at first. It was only when looking out of the kitchen window, that I had seen her frail body lying face down on the grass.

It was freezing outside. The middle of January in London has snow on the ground.

"What?" I had looked amazed that anyone would be outside as she was. The air temperature would have been below zero! (Thinking back now, though – it had probably been a ploy. She hadn't been that cold, so hadn't been out there that long!)

On seeing her, I had immediately dashed outside and woken her up. She had appeared groggy but obeyed me. Once inside, I had made her tea.

The second time I came home and found her asleep in the garden, I didn't immediately dash out to help her, I let her lie there for a while. (Wow, now I'm playing her games!) I had even decided to walk to the corner store to buy a biscuit to have with my coffee, but on reaching the road crossing leading to the store, I had felt pangs of guilt and had then immediately rushed home. It didn't matter how much I hated her, I couldn't leave her like that. I couldn't be responsible for causing her harm.

Flying back into the house and out into the garden, I had immediately flown back inside to call an ambulance. As soon as I had touched my mother, I had recognised that she was unconscious. She was also very cold this time, so had been out there for a while.

My father and I went to visit her that night in hospital. We were told that my mother had a cancerous tumour in her thyroid gland, and that it could be removed.

It was and she returned home a week later.

Not having a thyroid gland now, meant my mother needed to take thyroid tablets. She had always had an over-active thyroid gland, which was one of the reasons for her hyper-activity, so prevalent in everything she did, and one reason for her inability to relax, or allow us to either.

Once home, and on her treatment plan, my mother's behaviours became even more obsessive. She became obsessed with food. She didn't return to work immediately, but instead stayed home to bake her cakes. The first day after she had returned home from hospital, I came home straight from school to make sure she was all right.

"What are you doing?" I had asked her.

"I'm eating," she had looked up at me startled.

"What, all this?" I had looked aghast at the amount of food she had placed out on the table. She had spent the day baking a chocolate cake, a fruit cake, orange slices, a trifle, little butterfly cakes, scones and a malt loaf. Now, here she was at the table scoffing the lot!

Watching her eat, I estimated her calorie intake to be about five thousand.

When she saw my troubled expression, she said, "I now need

this much food every day."

So, imagine how I felt at that moment. Here was I deprived of any of these food items all my life, facing a woman who was stuffing her face gluttonously on all of them. (She intended to eat every crumb of cake and every splash of trifle – I was stunned!)

I couldn't stomach what I was watching. In my life now, the memory of that afternoon prohibits me from ever eating cake. I was never permitted this food choice as a child and so choose not to eat it as an adult.

My mother's sickness had been the turning point in my parent's marriage. Once his wife had returned home from her operation, my father had decided to change the way he lived. He and I together rearranged the house to make a family living room at the front, and a family rumpus room at the back that had a television and a games table. On returning home from work each night, he would join her in the front room to share their evenings together.

"Susie, I'd like us to have a family dinner at nights now. I'll give you food money, like I used to, so your mother doesn't have to cook," he had smiled at me.

My father got his way with changing the house around, but he didn't get his way with the family dinner.

How surprising!

My mother didn't mind her husband joining her at night in the front room, because most nights she preferred to go up to her little sewing room upstairs. That was her escape. That room had been my sister, Justine's, bedroom before she moved to Canada to live with our aunt.

My mother loved her little sewing room, but there was no way she was having me cook dinner each night. She had her cakes!

Believe in Yourself

Believe in yourself
And what you want to achieve
In your life.
Know who you are
And the reason you're here.
You set your own goals
And the directions you want
To achieve.
Restore your faith –
Let your passions run free.
You'll surprise yourself
At how talented you are
In all things.
Hold your head high –
Look the world in the eye.
Be happy with life,
And reflect this on others
Who need you,
So that they too
Can pursue who they are.

The Tunnel

From the time that I can remember, I have dreaded 'The Tunnel!' In my subconscious, I believed that this would happen when I was eighteen – the point I knew I would leave home and go to college. Little did I realise that I was about to enter that 'tunnel' now – at the age of thirteen!

A Typical Day

I awake around five a.m. I am exhausted – physically and emotionally. Last night, as I do every night, I put my fingers in my ears, hide under the bed covers and scream silently. I cannot scream aloud, which is what I really want to do. The tension I feel is so intense, that I feel my nerves stretching like thin pieces of elastic. My fear is that these thin strips will break, and I will lose my mind.

In my screaming, I cry savagely, oozing out every, last fragment of emotion from my body, as tears stream down my face. I start at ten p.m., when my mother has gone to bed, and I scream like this for four hours non-stop. I do this every night relentlessly, or I cannot survive the next day. I cannot risk coming to bed before this hour, for fear she will come in and find me. This infelicitous covert behaviour has become a way of life for me.

By ten p.m. both of my parents are sleeping. They share the large front bedroom, and Christine and I have the double back room. By two a.m. each night I am so exhausted that I drift into sleep for around three hours – never more than that – I can't, because I cannot risk being asleep when my mother wakes up. My bed, after four hours of crying, is soaking wet, but on waking is always dry again.

If I were to wake up around six a.m. when my father gets up to make tea, I would hear my mother coughing. On sipping her tea each morning, she would cough up her guts, bouts that would be extended retchings in which she would convulse for at least ten minutes. My nerves could not stand it. Only having three hours sleep each night did not give my nerves sufficient time to recover - hearing her coughing was worse than lacking sleep. So, I chose the lack of sleep.

I had also become increasingly intolerant of the other sounds that my mother made. She was in the habit of making a mouth noise with her teeth that again set my nerves on edge. To protect my nerves, I would keep my fingers in my ears at any time I felt in danger of hearing her whilst I was in bed. When I was up and about, I knew I had to bear it, and leave the house as soon as possible to avoid any further aggravation.

At five a.m. I get up quietly. I don't want anyone to hear me getting dressed and leaving the house. Most mornings I can leave and walk into Harrow, a distance of three miles, which takes me an hour. As it's February, the weather is cold. I can see my breath as I walk, but brisk walking soon warms me up. I don't have a jacket to wear, only my black jumper that I knitted, with my grey, school trousers and white shirt that I had found in a charity shop in Harrow. My school uniform was acceptable. Today, though, my plans are to be thwarted.

"You're not going to school today," my mother's voice comes from the kitchen. "I had a phone call from your principal last night. She told me you were caught cheating in a test, and that you must stay home until I meet with her this afternoon."

"What are you talking about?" I glare at my mother, as I open the kitchen door and see her sitting at the kitchen table drinking tea.

"Gosh, she got up quietly today – and she hasn't coughed yet. How devious of her," I think to myself. "She did not want me to hear her get up!"

"The principal said someone had told her you cheated in a test, and I have to meet with her today at four p.m."

My mind begins racing. I frantically search for anything that might give me a clue as to where this idea has come from. I certainly hadn't cheated in any test. Our exams had finished at the end of the year, and so far, we hadn't had any tests. Being in Year 8, the only tests we have are the half-yearly and yearlies. This whole process for reporting cheating, a school meeting and staying home from school didn't make sense to me. My instincts tell me, it's a ploy.

But what can I do? I can't leave and go up to the school. It is too early, but it is what I want to do.

"By eight thirty a.m. she will have organised my day to prevent me from going anywhere near the school. What is her game today?" I think worriedly to myself.

Since returning to school for this New Year, my mother had frequently kept me home from school. There were many excuses that she used. Having done well in my exams, she was determined to make sure I failed any further tests. Of course, she wasn't going up to the school at four p.m. I knew this was a lie. She never went anywhere near the school, and I hadn't heard her on the phone the night before.

"How can she lie so blatantly?" I think to myself. "Where does she hatch these plots from?"

"I've written you a list of jobs for today. As you will be home, you may as well be useful," her tone was low and emotionless.

Looking at the list, I think to myself, "She's been up all night, planning this!"

- Cleaning the silverware.
- Polishing the brassware.

- Scrubbing the backdoor steps.
- Vacuuming the house and dusting the surfaces.
- Cleaning out the cutlery drawer.
- Going up to the attic to sort out all the food stored up there into tins, packets and jars, and to place in the containers placed up there for this purpose ("Gosh, she must have planned this yesterday and bought containers," I stare fixedly at her piece of paper).
- Shopping list from North Harrow (these shops are in the opposite direction to my school, so I will have no opportunity to call in and see the principal).
- Dental appointment in Harrow at two thirty p.m.
- Visit Mr Walsh in Ruislip – get the train from Harrow to Ruislip and be there by four thirty p.m.

I look incredulously at the list. "She has planned every second of my day to avoid any chance of me going up to the school."

I look across at the woman, who is my mother. Most days I go along with her ways. I do as she says. I take the least line of resistance because the tension I feel is too great to challenge her every time she makes a move such as this one. But... not today!

Glaring rigidly into her face, I firmly stand my ground. "I cannot be absent from school today. I have two English classes to teach this morning and a French class this afternoon. I also have a netball game this afternoon after school."

"What do you mean you are teaching? Who are you teaching?" she hisses at me.

I hadn't told my mother about these lessons because it was my secret world, and I didn't want her destroying it. "Mrs Wall asked me to do some teaching."

"Well," she fumes, "We'll see about that! You are not going

to school today!"

"So, try and stop me!" I continue to glare at her.

My mother gets up immediately from her chair and stands between me and the door leading from the kitchen to the hall.

"Now, see if you can get out!" she smiles a wry smile at me.

Continuing to glare rigidly into her face, I move to brush past her, but every time I turn one way, she turns to counter my move. We play this game for several moments before I finally firmly take her arm and force it out of the way.

She attacks me full on, lunging at me with all her strength, raising her right hand to whack me, but I am primed. I lift my arms above my head to stop the whack and force her body backwards. As my left arm makes contact with her right arm, I see fear in her eyes. I continue to glare sternly into her face.

"I can hit you until you are eighteen years of age!" she snarls at me.

"Actually, you can't!" I snarl back. "Don't you ever attempt to do that to me again!"

I then push her out of the way and leave the room and the house.

Once outside, the cold air hits me, but it is refreshing and gives me a chance to calm my nerves. I walk briskly into Harrow scarcely daring to even think about this violent encounter and how she might be when I return home later that day.

"Drats," I think to myself, "I've left all my schoolbooks and netball gear at home. I can't go back and get them."

However, as I continue walking, I think to myself, "Why can't I go back and get them? I'm not going to let this woman bully me any more!"

Jogging back to the house, I sneak in the back door, dash up to my room and grab my things as quickly and as surreptitiously as I can. The house is very quiet. I breathe a sigh of relief. "She's gone back to bed."

Exiting the house once more, I feel much happier now about my day. I feel that I have won a significant victory over my mother. I will never forget that look of sheer fear on her face and in her eyes. She was scared of the power I now had over her. I didn't think she would try anything else today.

Looking back on that day, how wrong was I?

My first lesson had been English. Miss Sinclair, the teacher, had announced that some of us would be sitting the Oxford English 'O' Level Examination in English Language and Literature. She had said that we were good enough and it would be excellent preparation for the London Board later. In the U.K. there are three boards for these examinations that equate to a similar level of attainment to the Australian Higher School Certificate. It is usual to sit this level in Year 11 and then progress to the much more difficult 'A' Level Examinations in Year 12. To sit the Oxford Board in Year 8 was exciting. I knew that I would be chosen, and I secretly felt this would set me on a good pathway for Teacher's College.

My next lesson was Mathematics. Mr Parfitt, the teacher, also asked myself and three other girls if we would be interested in sitting the Oxford Pure Mathematics Examination. Of course, we were. *Today was going to be a great day*, I thought. How wrong was I?

After the morning break, I taught my two Year 7 English classes. There was never a teacher in the classroom at this time. It was as if I were the assigned teacher. I knew I was competent. I'd taught my sister's Year 3 class for several months when I was in Year 6, and I knew how to structure a lesson that provided practical and interesting activities for the students to enjoy learning. (In retrospect, I should have been a high school English teacher!)

The students liked me teaching them and they worked hard for me.

It was after lunch when it happened. My first lesson had been a double Biology lesson followed by a single Geography one. The last remaining session was my own class that I taught for French.

French was taught in the laboratory that had all glass windows down the side of the building that faced the school gardens. There was a pathway alongside these glass windows that led to a side door into the main building. Just as I was moving towards the side of the room, near the glass windows, I saw my mother charging along the pathway. I froze. "What the f _ _ _ is she doing here?" I hissed to myself.

I hadn't had a chance to visit the principal to ask her about my mother's supposed meeting. "Was she telling the truth?" I wondered. Fear and panic swelled inside me. No-one had said anything to me all day.

It was at that moment that she saw me through the glass. She could see that I was standing facing the windows. With one almighty blow, she smashed her right fist right through the glass to land me a punch on my nose. The impact of her punch and the glass sent me flying backwards into a row of student desks. I banged my back against these desks before falling to the ground. There was blood and glass everywhere.

Having delivered her punch, my mother had immediately left, not paying any more attention to me. She'd done what she had come to do.

The students in my class were really upset. The Mathematics teacher had heard the explosion and immediately come to investigate. He organised for the principal (Mrs Wall) to take the class for the remainder of the lesson, and for the class to move to a safe room, while I went to sick bay for medical treatment. I was shell-shocked. I was embarrassed. I had never been so embarrassed in my life.

Now, in my current life, I choose not to be embarrassed. Embarrassment is a choice emotion, and I choose not to be embarrassed. When you have experienced severe embarrassment, nothing else is ever so embarrassing again in your life! As a thirteen-year-old girl whose mother has just stormed into her teaching room and punched her in that vicious way, is more than embarrassing. My body went into shock for some time. My face was badly cut by the slivers of glass, some of which were embedded in my skin.

It had been my Biology teacher who had taken me to Harrow Hospital. The glass needed to be removed, and my face needed stitches. Miss Thorning, my teacher, had been lovely. She had stayed with me, chatted to me and bought me dinner. She had then taken me home afterwards, which was about ten p.m. I was so glad my mother had been in bed when I had walked in the door.

Going to bed that night, I wondered what plans my mother had for me tomorrow.

The next day at school I was required to meet with the principal. I asked her about the meeting with my mother, and she replied that she was not aware of any meeting. There was no investigation into this matter. Thinking about this incident – if it had happened in a school today, it would have been a major incident that warranted investigation, not just by the police, but also by child protection officers. In 1964, this incident had not even been recorded.

As the year progressed, I journeyed deeper and deeper into the tunnel. Each new day, brought varying ploys, plays and taunts orchestrated to cause me anguish, or grief of some kind. I never knew what was around the corner, even though I prepared myself for the worst every day. I could never relax. With only three hours sleep each night, my body had little time to recover from the previous day's episodes. Each night I was like a music box that had been wound up to maximum capacity and now had to be released. The only difference with a music box, is that this plays gentle, calming tunes, whereas my tune was an unfurling intensely silent scream.

As with all days and nights, I survived them the best way I could. The next day I did my lessons as if nothing had happened the previous day. No-one spoke to me about the incident, and I didn't initiate any conversation.

As Easter approached, I prepared for the Oxford examinations. Only a small group of us had been selected to sit these papers, and we all felt very special. It was a wonderful feeling having this academic challenge.

I scored 100% in both the written and oral French components, I scored an A in the English Language Paper and an A- in the English Literature Paper. In Mathematics, I scored an A for Geometry, an A- for Algebra and a B+ for Arithmetic. I was pleased with my results.

It was after Easter that I began to seriously lose my focus, though. My survival strategies worked Mondays to Thursdays, but from Friday afternoon to Monday morning, the black curtain of doom descended around me. The more I tried to escape the house, the more my mother jeered and ridiculed me. After the window incident, she had been determined to reclaim the power she had lost that day. She never let up and she never tired of her taunts. She knew I loathed her, and so she played me more.

During the remainder of Year 8 from Easter to July, I became increasingly depressed. My nerves tightened and I was fearful of any of them snapping. By Fridays with the weekends looming, my gloomy mood would be noticed at school. I had no escape on Friday nights, as my mother knew I had no urgent essays to write. Not being permitted to do any schoolwork at home, I found my marks and focus slipping even further. I couldn't concentrate in class – I was too tired, and too mentally and physically exhausted to care any more. Part of me wanted to give up and part of me refused to let go of the slightest single strand of nerve. I felt that if I let go of one, I feared they would all crumble, and I would totally lose control of my mind.

"Sue, why don't you come to France with me for a few weeks over the summer?" my father had come to me one day.

I couldn't believe it. I had been seriously worried how I would survive these six weeks off school. "Yes, I'll come," I had smiled grateful at him.

Between France and my friend Lynne, I managed to get through the weeks, being so grateful when the next school year started. France had been fun because, like my father, I had free First-Class fares and meals anywhere I travelled on ferries or trains. I loved the continental trains. Even to this day, I love travelling on the fast inter-city trains.

It wasn't long after school started that my parents were called to Canada to bring my sister home. Her weight had plummeted to thirty six kilos and my aunt feared she needed medical intervention. My sister Justine had gone to live with my father's sister for two years, because she had found living with my mother too difficult for her. (Justine was never a target for my mother's taunts, but being the oldest, she struggled to forge her way through her teenage years. She hated not being allowed to wear stockings, or a bra or teenage clothes, as her friends did. She struggled with not being allowed to go out with her friends. Our aunt had suggested she live with her for a while, which solved Justine's problem. Well, yes and no. The aftermath of her rape combined with her low self-esteem and neglect, left her emotionally vulnerable).

During the time that Justine lived with our aunt, she developed anorexia nervosa. Not much of this condition was known at the time. My aunt had certainly become concerned when Justine had become so ill, she wasn't eating anything. Panicking, and not wanting her niece's death on her hands, she had ordered my parents to come and fetch her. (My mother only went because my aunt had insisted).

They were away for three weeks, which for me meant that I had the house to myself for this time. I was so happy – I was so relieved – to have this reprieve was wonderful – yes, I felt for my sister because I knew that she struggled with her own self-concept. Justine had cared more than I did about our mother calling us fat and ugly, and that she didn't love either of us.

So, now I had these three weeks to myself. I could relax at night and have a break from my night-time traumas. It wasn't all plain sailing, though. In one of my earlier stories in this book, I relay a situation with the school counsellor that happened during this time. I had just turned fourteen and in Year 9 at school. Whilst in Year 8, I had known my mother had orchestrated the assault I experienced one night, whilst walking home from Lynne's house, and I secretly suspected that she had set up this counsellor one too. At the time I had thought it odd that the man had 'assumed' that I had known why he had visited. "What conversations did my mother have with these people that led them to think that they could sexually assault me?" (That was clearly their intent!)

There was another incident that I have never divulged to anyone, that also happened during these three weeks, but as I couldn't know for certain if my mother had choreographed these events, I have kept this incident hidden in my memory. (Hidden - yes, but not forgotten).

I will never forget the night before my parents and Justine arrived home from Canada. I think I felt such fear for what was to come, that I went into shock. Lying in bed, my mind went blank. I was conscious and yet not conscious, and my body was calm on the outside and yet in turmoil on the inside.

Drifting off to sleep I had awakened an hour later to find I had wet the bed – wow! How did that happen? "Great, now you have to spend the night washing sheets!" I had castigated myself. Not only did I wash the sheets, but I washed everything else in the house in readiness for my family's return, which they did shortly after I'd finished. Did they notice? No. The house had never been so clean nor would be again!

And so, my life resumed. Justine was organised to spend a few weeks in a medical facility, something she was happy about, as she hadn't wanted to return to the family house. Once her health had improved, she announced that she and Dave would be getting married. Dave had been her boyfriend before she had left for Canada and had faithfully waited for her return.

My mother had not enjoyed her overseas trip. She had hated living in my aunt's house. She had resented the imposition of being forced away from her home. Her frustrations and annoyance she took out on me. I found my schoolwork suffering badly, and my school report reflected this, something that had pleased my mother but concerned my father.

Now with Christmas looming, I became fearful of what to expect. I was jealous of Justine. Not only had she escaped to Canada for two years, but she was now escaping to a married life. Me, well, my life hung by a thread. At this point in time in my life, I too was suffering from weight loss, a lack of energy and chronic fatigue from lack of consistent quality sleep. My nighttime screaming had recommenced, and my nerves were gradually falling away to a point where I felt I was on the verge of a nervous breakdown – but I couldn't tell anyone.

Christmas Eve 1964

I spent the day in Harrow buying gifts for my family. My aunt in Canada had sent me some money to buy them all something. I'm thinking that she and my mother must have had some conversations about what went on in our house. My aunt always said to me that, "Your mother only ever had one daughter - and that wasn't either Justine or you!"

I knew that!

Tonight, I worry if I will survive the weekend ahead. What will my escape plan be? I think about how she has verbally attacked me today. She had yelled abuse at me so vile, that I cannot repeat her cruel words. She hadn't made any more moves to hit me, something I was prepared for if she did, having decided I would no longer accept these physical assaults. When she started these taunts, I would send a message to my brain to switch off my hearing. I became clever at tuning out some external sounds, so that I could see her lips moving, see her facial expressions, but not hear all the words she was yelling. This technique, however, would leave me with chronic migraine afterwards, and mental exhaustion.

It's now midnight. I'm half-way through my nightly ritual and I suddenly break down irretrievably.

"I can't go on like this," I sob silently. "I can't keep doing this every night."

I feel a sudden urge to get a knife – the largest, longest, sharpest one I can find, find my mother and stab her viciously in the chest. I want to see her blood flowing out, and I want to see her face as she realises her time is up. I feel such hatred in those few moments, that I scare myself.

"Where did all that come from?" I straighten up my legs and lie on my back in my bed. I look up at the ceiling. My sister is sleeping soundly, as she does every night. "Why is it that some people sleep well, and some do not? Even in the pitch blackness of the room, I can still make out the ceiling patterns. They calm me a little. I've thought about taking my own life many times, but I have never carefully planned the strategy. Now, here I was at fourteen years of age, planning to end my life.

I have a problem. It is my problem and only I can find a solution. It is interesting to realise that when you find the solution, it all seems so easy, so logical that you wonder why you haven't enacted the solution before. Of course, ending my life makes sense. It solves my problem. I feel euphoric as I drift off to sleep.

"Wake up!"

Someone is shaking me.

"Wake up!"

The shaking comes again.

I'm awake. Wide awake – suddenly. There's no-one else in my room. "Who is yelling at me, and who is shaking me?" I ask myself as my brain and body come as one to work out what is going on.

"Shalana, it is I, Ahman, your spirit guide."

I again stretch my legs out and lie flat on my back. This time

I have my eyes closed and I sense the presence of someone. (This was the first time I met my main spirit guide. I have two guides and since that time have met both souls many times through Past Life Regression or through Life Between Lives).

Lying in bed at this time, however, I wasn't scared by this experience, but I did recognise the importance of Ahman's visitation to me this night.

Shalana is my spiritual name.

"Shalana, you are here on Earth to be a teacher, and a teacher you will be. You will be the best teacher you can be. I am here to guide and protect you and to make sure that you succeed in your life goals during this lifetime. You have hard lessons to learn in this life. Each one of these lessons will help you grow in soul. You will become a strong, person who is able to withstand much hardship in your life. Every life has a purpose. You cannot give up your life now."

Ahman left and I slept.

On waking on Christmas Day, my heart felt lighter, I felt purpose again in my life.

Now, I just had to survive this day.

I was still in the tunnel, and I would be for several years to come. Prior to Ahman's conversation, I had reached a point in this dark journey where I thought I couldn't survive. I knew I was having a nervous breakdown and accelerating out of control to a point of no return. When I had found my solution, I had felt elated; I had felt finally that I was in control and could cope. Ahman's words had come in my sleep and awakened my mind and my senses. I now knew I had someone to help me. At any time I needed to talk, I knew he would be there.

My journey through the tunnel from that night onwards became slightly lighter; I knew life would still be difficult, but I now had a strong purpose – and a friend – and that made all the difference!

Happy Christmas!

Having met my spirit guide, I now knew that there was some reason why I wasn't supposed to experience a happy, loving family relationship in this lifetime. I would not be the person I am today if my childhood had been loving and supportive. It is the incredible hardship that I suffered daily, that has given me the energy to take on the challenges that have presented themselves to me in this lifetime. By succeeding in these challenges is what has helped me grow in spirit.

I'm still jealous, though, of girls who have lovely, caring mums! And I always will be – in this lifetime.

Pathways

We all choose the next path that we take,
And must then accept where that path leads.
We can't blame others for mistakes we've made
But instead learn the lessons from these misdeeds.
Some pathways are hard and challenge our might,
Whilst others become slippery and winding in part.
Be sure to be careful of what lies ahead
And always remember to follow your heart.
Our lives are a journey of pathways to find.
Each wrong turn will teach us lessons to learn.
So, when you come to the end of your days,
All glory in Heaven is yours to affirm.

The Great Escape

Returning to school after Christmas, I gradually began to find my focus and my zest for learning again. My slide had started midway through Year 8, just after sitting the Oxford examinations, and continued into 1965 until I could find myself again. I had been in a very dark hole for a long time, and I knew it would not be easy to recoup my confidence and self-esteem. With Ahmad watching over me, I knew that I was now not alone, and this comforted me.

This next era of my life, I call 'The Great Escape.' And it was...

There are many people who refute the presence of 'spirit' but, when you have experiences, you know. In all the books that I have written I have recounted stories of how spirit has intervened in critical situations in my life, or when I have been in the presence of a spirit soul for some purpose. For those sceptics, I can only hope that you do have an experience at least once in your lives, because it is such an amazing privilege.

I certainly believe that it was Ahman who was responsible for opening the door to the opportunities that presented themselves early on in this year, and then continued to present themselves until I began Year 11 in 1967. The first of these was the Duke of Edinburgh Award Scheme. Prince Philip, the Duke of Edinburgh had initiated a new scheme for young people to develop their leadership and community participation. Although this scheme was open to anyone from the age of fourteen, it was not designed to be an easy course to complete. This scheme still operates today, and in the same way that the three levels of Bronze, Silver and Gold become increasingly more difficult to complete, culminating in a very difficult outdoor expedition that must be successfully achieved as part of the Gold Award Level.

I commenced the Bronze Level in 1965 and completed the Gold Level in 1966. This program gave me opportunities to do activities in the community, other than nursing. I worked at aged-care centres, children's residential care centres, Sunday Schools and for Harrow Council teaching Cycling Proficiency. It gave me places to go at the weekends and holiday periods. I especially enjoyed working in the children's home in Tunbridge Wells at Christmas time.

Many of the children who came to stay in this home for short periods of time, had come from abusive family circumstances. This holiday time was respite for them, and it gave Community Services time to find them foster families. I was surprised one time, when two boys from an African background were asked to remove their clothes for a bath, that they had no concept of what a bath was and were fearful of removing any item of clothing. I found this sad that these two boys, aged eight and ten, had never taken a bath before.

In this children's home, I had a natural ability for this kind of work. For some of the time I worked there, I was assigned a little four-year-old whose mother had been sent to prison for fraud. John, my charge, had been placed in a cot, dummy in his mouth and wearing nappies that were soiled and hadn't been changed. It was my job to teach him to walk, talk, wee and poo, all of which he did very quickly.

Once the school term recommenced, I would travel to Tunbridge Wells every weekend to look after him and teach him how to formulate his words. When he was finally reunited with his mother, he was five years old, walking, talking and in control of his toileting. He was a regular little kid, ready for school.

I wrote him a poem. At this time in England there was a television show called, 'Castles in the Air.' This program was for children from foster homes. Their castles were their dreams.

Castles in the Air

Happy are those children that have railways in the hall,
Painting in the kitchen and stories when they're small.
Friends to come and visit them - ribbons for their hair,
To so many lonely children is a *'Castles in the Air.'*
Mothers doing washing up - neighbours picking flowers,
Brothers under motorcars for hours upon hours.
Coming home from school each day knowing someone's there,
To so many orphaned children is a *'Castles in the Air.'*
Can you think how it would be if all you could recall,
Were angry words and tempers, or no-one there at all?
Birthdays, picnics, Christmases - families that care,
To so many battered children is a *'Castles in the Air.'*
Sometimes kids are fortunate 'cos people can be found
To foster them and care for them, and always be around.
All these families ever ask is just a chance to share
With all these precious children their *'Castles in the Air.'*
They give them homes and firesides - railways in the hall,
Painting in the kitchen and stories when they're small.
They let their friends come visiting - buy ribbons for their hair,
But most of all they help them find their *'Castles in the Air.'*
To my beautiful little blue-eyed, fair-haired boy who had such dreams!

At last, I could escape my mother at this really, difficult holiday time, as well as weekends. My mother did not seem to mind me leaving the house for any reason. She liked having the house to herself, and so if I stayed overnight in the children's home, she had all weekend to herself. Our relationship improved during this time. I loved the home and the staff really liked me being with the children.

Another opportunity that came my way just after Easter, was The French Exchange Program. For the next two summers I spent two months each year living with a French family in Lyon, south of Paris. I enjoyed my time with this family and spoke French easily to them. I was fluent in speaking colloquially, which was good for them as their English was not easy to understand. They liked that I could speak French.

So, with my summers and Christmases organised, my life became a little easier to manage. I had things to look forward to that I knew helped me to survive the times I dreaded most. My frayed nerves began to repair themselves and I felt mentally stronger. The weekends were still difficult, but so long as I kept to my schedule of planned activities and didn't allow my mother to commandeer my time, I knew I could survive and tolerate the short amounts of time I spent at home.

Later in the year I went Outward Bound.

I loved Outward Bound! If there was ever an outdoor challenge program that suited me perfectly, it was this one!

This opportunity came to me through Harrow Council. They recognised my ability as a leader within the Cycling Proficiency Program and had awarded me the grandiose title of 'Assistant

Road Safety Officer for Harrow Council.' They offered me a sponsorship to undertake the Outward-Bound Challenge, even though I was too young at the time. The earliest entry is sixteen years of age, but I was granted special permission.

This four-week course, located in North Wales, is designed specifically for young people in the workplace, who aspire to becoming leaders in their fields. Most of the participants on my course were aged between twenty-three to twenty-five years of age. I was the only school student and the youngest ever to complete the course.

Outward Bound is a leadership building initiative in which participants are exposed to high level physical and mental challenges, especially challenges that involve problem-solving. There was also a public-speaking challenge, something most of the other participants hated, dreaded and made a big fuss about. The other aspect of the program that most participants hated, was using Nature's latrines!

When one is trekking across the countryside and climbing up Welsh mountains, one does not expect to turn a corner and find a pristine lavatory! I had just laughed as they trekked off furtively with their trowels and little bits of toilet paper.

This challenge course consisted of three levels of expedition. By the time we reached the Final Expedition, most of the group had become acclimatised, not just to the toileting arrangements, but also to the difficulties encountered abseiling down steep slopes, hiking up, across and down mountainous gorges or slipping through dark, dank potholes to find an underground course, brought.

Of course, I loved it! I excelled. I was physically and mentally strong enough to accept any challenge this program threw at me! I found everything easy.

In undertaking the Final Expedition, I was selected as the group leader for my little band of five – all other groups had six participants. As an added, bonus for my group alone, we were challenged by the Welsh Army Training School to reach Home Base first. There were no prizes, just the glory of winning.

At first, the lads had laughed at the idea that girls, who were not Army trained, could possibly outsmart and out-trek them.

After seeing us out on the slopes, miles ahead of them, however, they had laughed on the other side of their cheeks!

I had my group up each night at one thirty a.m. By two a.m. we had scoffed our breakfast, packed up our campsite, taken all the compass bearings for the day's trek and were already on our way. Even our instructor had been caught napping when she had awoken at four a.m. and found us long gone. The next night she learned not to sleep!

Yes, we beat the boys! I trained my troupe well. They trusted my judgment as well as my ability to make good decisions. By the end of the course, we had become firm friends. This final expedition qualified me for the Gold Duke of Edinburgh Award, which I received from Prince Philip at Buckingham Palace soon after arriving home from Outward Bound.

All these extra-curricula activities strengthened my confidence and developed better levels of self-esteem. I had always led a juxta positional existence: at home having no worth – in the community being well thought of. I accepted this and tried hard not to let my home life destroy the good things that were happening at this time.

So, as 1966 closed, I closed my eyes with relief as I lay in bed in the children's home. I had a haven to go to – somewhere where I felt safe, welcome and where I was needed. I have an affinity with children. They warm to me readily and feel safe. I hoped this New Year would continue to be good for me. Thank you, Ahman.

Returning to school after the Christmas break, I had the rest of my 'O' levels to complete. Like many of my friends, we were taking these examinations early. It was usual to sit them at the end of Year 11. We were in Year 10, but we had already sat some of the Oxford Board tests, and so our teachers had decided we were ready for this academic challenge. I studied hard and took nine subjects at this level. This put me in good stead for any university course of my choice. Once we had finished this battery of tests, we went out on Work Experience for the remaining four weeks of the school year.

This was my next escape, and it was something else I loved. The husband of my Economics teacher was the secretary for a publishing company in London, and he agreed to let me work in his office. I learned how to use the switchboard, set up meetings with authors and publishing staff, and type letters. I enjoyed the office life, but I knew it would not be my chosen career path, as I disliked the confines of the office. I did, however, like meeting the authors of children's books, as well as many of the writers of non-fiction books - the two areas of publishing that this company specialised in.

As well as working during the week in London, I now worked at the weekends for Maynard Confectioners. This company was famous in England for making wine gums. They also made liquorice all sorts and other types of sweets. I did not particularly enjoy the long, laborious hours spent weighing copious quantities of lollies, but it did give me a little pocket money. On one occasion, a Sunday, I felt privileged to serve a young man who came in to buy chocolate and a drink. I recognised him as a famous musician - he had recorded many pop chart hits.

As he had left the shop, he had smiled at me and said, "I shouldn't really, but I can't resist!" He had referred to the chocolate.

This confectionery shop was in Pinner, Middlesex, where his family lived at the time. Pinner was only a short walk from North Harrow, where I lived. Many famous people lived in Pinner, including Reginald Dwight, who changed his name to Elton John. He was born in Pinner Green, a place I would frequently walk to when I wanted to clear my head and enjoy the country aspects of suburban life. Pinner was a much prettier place to walk than downtown Harrow.

My last great escape was to the Himalayas with Outward Bound. I had been selected as part of an elite group of twenty hikers to trek the mountain trails of Nepal. The expedition was an introduction to snow and ice climbing, something I had not experienced before. There were ten senior instructors, who led us to the top of Mera Peak, which is about two thousand metres lower than Mount Everest.

I was apprehensive about this expedition, as I knew I was the youngest person to be selected for such an elite trek. Each year Outward Bound chose their best twenty participants, and I had felt honoured to be selected.

The expedition lasted three glorious weeks, and for me it was a significant achievement, and it ended my Great Escape.

Having been through my own inner struggles with suicide, I was deeply saddened when my daughter wrote this poem when she felt this was her only option.

The Memory of Loneliness

Have you ever felt so empty within you that life ceases to exist?
To wake in the morning and hear my silence -
A silence that offends me more than most obtrusive noise.
Memories serve to inflict the pain of history
Rekindling thoughts of friends once trusted, or lovers once adored.
My constant daily struggle to find the solace within
Dies into the night as tears disappear into my pillow.
I will awake again – but not really!
My eyes will open to a clouded view of humanity,
One which I cannot cast aside – this is my reality.
This midnight hour forgives all who render themselves helpless,
But beware the relentless break of dawn.
Like the perfect storm the collaboration of energy
Can illuminate a night sky.
At this hour my mind is poisoned by thoughts of loathing,
Self-pity and unrest.
Cascading visions – more like daylight nightmares
Filtering life's light until there is nothing left to see
But hatred and sorry excuses.
These memories my soul never left behind.

Cally

To my lovely daughter, who is my best friend

A Mother's Response

Loathing and pity are the soul's worst enemies
For they destroy our inner ego.
We all respond to words of kindness and love,
Even if not meant fully at the time.
They are good for our soul to hear.
We all feel loneliness at times –
To be alone is frightening.
We all take what we can from life and still want more,
For it is in nature to do so.
Our patience though is to give to others
All manner of love and kindness,
So that we grow in spirit.
Cally - know we are never really
Alone.
One day your soul will seek and find those memories
Your heart has left behind,
For each of us has borne all manner of pain,
Loneliness, deceit and fear.
Yes – fear is the real killer,
As our hearts forgive so easily
Yet still at the end of the day –
Our soul remembers!

The Conversation

In my current life I am a teacher. I started teaching in 1972 at Gray's Comprehensive School in Essex as a Geography, Health and Physical Education specialist. I taught for more than thirty years in secondary education before transferring to the Kindergarten to Year 12 arena. I enjoy teaching primary-age children more than high school students because I know I can make a difference to how they perceive their academic potential. I would have loved to have had a teacher who had nurtured my academic ability instead of always feeling worthless about myself.

Once students have a good perception about themselves, they develop confidence. This is the single, most important aspect of knowing you can achieve anything you set out to do. And you can! At seventeen years of age, I could not see this! I did not believe this!

I know from this teaching experience that most students enjoy school more as they progress to the higher echelons. The senior years are always more engaging as teachers generally prefer to teach senior students. Having sat all my pre-requisite examinations, I could take on other activities in Year 11.

From the onset of the year in September 1967, I was elected Senior Prefect. My school had a strong leadership team and believed in the ethos of promoting leadership skills in girls. It was at a time when women were beginning to have greater work options in their career paths, and not just expected to stay home and be housewives. As the Senior Prefect, it was my job to assist the playground duty teachers during the school breaks. I remember on one occasion, a substitute teacher had asked a group of girls to vacate the toilets, and they had refused to comply, but then one look from me and they had all left quietly. The teacher had just looked at me. It was the way it was. (I've always had 'the look!')

Once my senior subjects were all organised, the principal, again asked me to teach French and English to the junior students. I enjoyed teaching and I knew it was where my career lay. I was also able to take up the Pitman Shorthand Typing Course, which was offered to students in Years 11 and 12. I could have chosen the State Enrolled Nursing Course (S.E.N.) but this career path did not interest me. Neither did becoming a secretary, but I felt the typing skills would be useful.

Shorthand was difficult at first but became easier as I became more familiar with all the symbols and how to place them with the vowels above, on or below the lines. It was like learning a foreign language. Part of this course required me to undertake work experience in several different types of offices, all of which I hated and felt trapped. However, at the completion of the course, I had attained a good typing speed and could take notes using shorthand to a satisfactory level.

Now that I was in Year 11, I was invited to participate in the Senior Social Club. This was a social club for Year 11 girls from my school to get together with the Year 11 boys from their school next door. We met each Friday night in the gymnasium to play badminton. Here I met Brian. Brian asked me out on the first night of the get together and we stayed best friends for nine months. Once we had connected, we did everything together. He carried my books home from school, bought me coffee after school, took me out at the weekends, invited me to tea with his family and gave me gifts. He was a sweetie! He stood over six feet four inches tall and was athletic in build. He was perfect.

I started going out with Brian in November 1967 and ended our relationship in August 1968 after, 'The Conversation.'

Brian never came into my house. He would always drop and kiss and leave. It was a Saturday night, when dropping me off at my house, he had quietly said, "I had a conversation with your mother today."

"What," I had looked at him aghast. "When was this?"

I had been at work at Maynard Confectioners in North Harrow all day. Brian had walked up to meet me at about 5.15 p.m. that night, and we had gone to the cinema to watch a film. He hadn't said anything to me until he had dropped me off.

"Your mother asked me to come for tea this afternoon at four p.m.," Brian looked nervously at me.

"And you never told me?" I looked incredulously at him.

"I thought you knew," he looked even more nervously at me.

"But you knew I was at work, so why would you go without me?" I stared right at him, becoming now agitated at the thought that my mother had plotted some ploy or scheme I didn't know about.

Yes, she had schemed. I'll come back to this conversation.

Just before Easter of this year, I had met Michael. I had been invited to my neighbour's twenty-first birthday party, and Michael and I had talked and connected. He was a nice young man, and he asked me out for dinner. We went to Windsor to an Indian restaurant and then walked by the river. It was a lovely evening, except that I felt ill from what I had been given to eat. I had ordered a chicken curry, but as I was eating it, I had felt that it wasn't. I survived the car trip back home but was violently ill as soon as I opened the front door. (I knew I'd eaten cat!)

When you are on a date, though, and you're not paying, you don't say anything. I only went out with Michael one more time. He organised for his family to be out one Saturday night, and so we had the house to ourselves. I had just sat down on his sofa, when he suddenly got down on one knee and asked me 'that question.'

I was shocked. I was seventeen years old, I still had eighteen months of school remaining and I was planning to go to college – getting married was the furthest thing from my mind.

"Michael, I can't marry you. I'm too young," I had looked at him.

"I know," he had smiled at me. "I'll wait for you. I'll wait six years for you. You can go to college and take as long as you like to get your qualifications, and I'll be here waiting. I won't go out with anyone else if I know you'll marry me."

"Michael, that's not fair to you. I can't do that to you. I don't know where my life will take me in the future," I smiled kindly at him. "I think I should go home."

Lying in bed that night I had felt immensely sorry for this young man. He was twenty-four years of age and was already an Assistant Bank Manager. He had a great career path ahead of him, and now just wanted his wife. He had gone to such trouble to organise 'the setting.'

I smiled. No-one had ever gone to such trouble for me before, and it was really, nice. I felt special. I knew that I couldn't marry him, though because I didn't feel that way about him.

Now back to Brian.

"Brian, why didn't you say anything to me earlier?"

Putting his arms around my neck and body, he had just held me close and very tight. Being so tall, his body had enveloped me, covering my head and shoulders, so that I could scarcely breathe. I sensed something was savagely wrong, and I was fearful of what my mother had done.

"I couldn't," he finally said. "I didn't know how to tell you. It was all so awful."

Brian had then started crying. I released his hold on me and looked at the tears falling down his cheeks.

"We need to talk, but now is not the right time. It's too cold out here. We can meet after work tomorrow."

Brian had then left, and I had gone to bed. The house had been quiet at that hour, but I sensed evil in the air.

As suggested, Brian duly met me at the Pinner Maynard shop, where I worked until four p.m. on Sundays. Looking at me as I had closed the shop door, he had smiled nervously. Neither of us spoke. I didn't want to speak. I didn't want to listen to his talking. I didn't want to know what my mother had done or said. I just knew I had to know. We strolled across to a park, where we could sit in a gazebo. Most of the families picnicking were beginning to head home, and we could now have our private chat.

"What happened Brian?"

She asked me into the living room where we sat and drank tea.

My mother: Brian why are you going out with my daughter, when you know she is not interested in you, but in another young man that she is going to marry?

"Your mother looked right across at me in a scowling way."

Brian looked at me visibly shaking. I could see that he was confused now about our relationship.

"Brian, I am not going to marry anyone. I'm going to college next year. You know about Michael, and I'm not going out with him any more. Just tell me the script." He had my attention, and

I was now fearful of any plan my mother had in mind.

My mother: Brian, you seem a nice young man, much too nice for my daughter. Susan doesn't deserve you. You should find a pretty, young girl more suited to you. Susan is fat and lazy, and good for nothing. She will not make you a good wife. She is only nice to you while you are dating, but you will see the real 'her' when you get to know her better.

Brian: Mrs Makeham I have been going out with Sue for quite a while. We met last November, and we've been inseparable since. My parents love her and want us to be friends.

My mother: Brian, you don't get my drift. You are not to go out with Susan any more. She is a horrible person, who is not good for you. She is greedy and selfish, and she will take all your money.

Brian: Mrs Makeham, Sue is the one who pays for what we do now. She is the generous one. I do not have a job and so cannot afford to buy our movie tickets. She is wonderful to me, and I want to keep going out with her.

"At this point your mother became extremely agitated and began fidgeting. Her eyes became angry, and I was worried what she would do or say next. I was so shocked by what she was saying to me."

Brian looked across at me and squeezed my hand.

My mother: You do not know Susan. She is a nasty, spiteful, vicious, conniving person, who will do anything she can to get you to marry her, and then she will take all your money.

"Your mother had then stood up and yelled at me, standing over me in a threatening way."

My mother: You are not to see Susan again. Do you hear me?

"I was frightened. She was so angry. She looked mad for a

moment, and then she calmed down."

My mother: Brian let's have some tea. Here try some of my malt loaf.

"We both sat silent for a while, and then she said:

My mother: You know Brian, Susan told me that she is going to break it off with you. She said she doesn't really like you and is only going out with you because she has no-one else - or didn't until Michael came along.

Brian: She told me she doesn't want to go out with Michael. She's not interested in him.

My mother: You stupid boy – she lied.

Your mother had then screamed these words at me in a sudden fly of fury."

Brian: I, I, I think, I'd better go.

"I stood to leave, but she blocked the door. I couldn't get out."

My mother: You are not leaving this house until you tell me you will never see my daughter again!

"Her words were fierce and powerful, and I felt intimidated. What could I do? I said I would end our relationship."

At this point in our conversation, Brian cupped his face in his hands and began crying uncontrollably. I felt immensely sorry for him. I had put up with my mother's brutality all my life, but he had only been subjected to an hour of it. He hadn't been expecting to be bullied or told such terrible things about his girlfriend, and he hadn't expected to be told to end the relationship. I was his first girlfriend, whereas I had gone out with other boys.

For most of my childhood I had been friends with a boy called Graham. Graham had been the son of one of my father's work colleagues, and we had formed a close friendship over the years, seeing each other when we could. When I was sixteen, we had been sitting in a pub one Sunday night when he had asked me to marry him. He had expected me to say yes, but I had said no. We had still remained friends. Our relationship had always been platonic, and I had wanted it to stay that way. When Graham finally did meet his wife to be, I was amused that she was exactly like me.

Brian and I held each other that afternoon until the cool of the evening air got the better of us. I would not let him walk me home. We said our farewells and I had said, "Don't believe those things she said about me."

"Sue, she said things to me I cannot repeat to you. I was shocked by what she said. Of course, I don't believe them, but how can I go out with you now?"

"I know," we had kissed and parted. I never saw Brian again.

It had been the following Sunday when the next conversation happened. As Brian had not met me after work, I had come straight home. My mother wasn't expecting me home so early. It was just on five p.m. when I opened the door, and Michael was just leaving the house. Seeing my mother and Michael standing in the hallway, I had immediately understood her plan. My only question was, 'How had she found out Michael's contact number?'

At no time had I given her his home contact details or anything about him.

In writing up my life story, the one thing that stands out for me, is how devious my mother had been in all the schemes and plots she connived. One of my failings was to recognise the tortuous nature of her plans. Looking back, I can see that she must have plotted for several days, possibly weeks, beforehand before orchestrating any scheme. I had just accepted what had happened at any one time, without realising the significance of the depth of plot that had been implemented.

In this latest ploy, she had contacted Brian and Michael without my knowledge and invited them to clandestine meetings with her, each for a different purpose. Her meeting with Brian had been to force him to end our relationship, whereas the meeting with Michael had a different agenda.

"Michael, why are you here?" I had asked him as I saw him standing next to my mother. She, of course, had been really annoyed that I had walked in at that moment. She had been really annoyed, too, that I had left with him that afternoon.

"Michael let's get some coffee from the service station and you can tell me what is going on," I had quietly said to him.

As we sat in his little, red Coupe that afternoon sipping our coffees, we talked.

"Michael, I don't know how my mother found out your personal contact details, nor do I know why you accepted her invitation. Did you think I was going to be there?"

"No, I knew you were at work."

"So, why did you go?"

"Because I want to marry you, and I thought your mother might persuade you."

"So, did you contact her?" I looked incredulously at him.

"No, but when she asked me to come over for tea, I thought that this was the agenda. I thought you knew and were okay with it."

"Michael, my mother only likes you because you are an Assistant Bank Manager, and she sees prospects for your career. I don't want to know what the conversation was that you had with my mother. It's none of her business. It's not even your business to talk to my mother about me and what I'm going to do in the future.

I'm not interested in whether you are going to be a bank manager or something else. I'm much more interested in you as a person, and at this time in my life, I am not interested in getting married to anyone, let alone you. I am much too young, and I have my career ahead of me. Yes, I like you, but I'm not in love with you because I don't even know what that means yet."

We had both sat in his car for quite some time before he finally said, "I'll drive you home."

Sitting outside my house, it was now getting late. My mother would be watching television and my father would be listening to his music. I crept in and went to bed.

There would be no more conversations about this matter.

The 'Meaning of Life'

We are all born equal,
Is that not so?
But how do we know this –
How can we know?
Imagine a diamond
Inside our heart,
Unpolished, discoloured –
Shining in part.
The more we help others
To learn and to love,
The more that our diamond
Shines above.
It takes many lifetimes
To reach the stage
Where our little diamond
Lights up the page.
Our soul is our diamond,
Our love of life.
It grows deep inside us
Releasing strife.
Our soul grows much brighter,
Reflecting rays,
Revealing talents
In many ways.
In harmony with nature,

A course now run,
A lifetime of journeys
Ends now – it's done.

The Final Curtain

Our lives are a carousel – each day that passes we go round in circles as we ride the painted ponies. We laugh at the highs, and we cry at the lows.

Carousel

Our lives are like a carousel.
We take the ride and keep on turning
Round and round until we find
The perfect partner.
We may get off to find our love,
But make mistakes, but keep on going
Around and around, until we find
What we think we want.
Are we happy on this ride,
Or have we made the same mistakes
Time after time, or do we fall
For more of the same?
We must be strong and trust our horse.
He knows just when it's time to ride
Around and around until he spots
Our perfect partner.
So, sit back and enjoy the ride.

Our lives are equally a rollercoaster, that can be both amazing and terrifying at the same time. Most of my life on the rollercoaster was terrifying. I knew that at the time, but I also knew I had to survive.

It was Winston Churchill* who said, *'If you're going through hell, keep going.'*

He also said, *'This is the lesson: never give in, never give in, never, never, never, never—in nothing, great or small, large or petty—never give in except to convictions of honour and good sense.'*

*Winston Churchill was England's Prime Minister from 1940 – 1945 and from 1951 – 1955.

No, I would never give in. It is what held my last strand of nerve attached to me during my breakdown when I was fifteen. I had been so fearful of it breaking, causing me to lose my mind. But … I hung on.

I knew that my life was much harder than some people's lives. I met children, who I knew, came from impoverished backgrounds, or were subjected to physical or sexual abuse. I felt for those children as I felt for myself. I knew I could never disclose any aspect of my life to anyone because they would not have believed me. The hardest thing about emotional abuse, is that it does not carry scars that can be seen in the way physical scars make their mark. My visible scars could be seen in my demeanour, appearance and disposition, but to the untrained observer, these could not, and were not interpreted as warranting attention or treatment. In 1969 people did not recognise the outward signs of emotional abuse in the same way professionals, such as teachers or doctors, are trained to observe and act today.

I had very low self-esteem and a poor self-image. I walked with my nose on my knees, never wanting to face the world. I could never look at myself in the mirror. Even though I was Head Girl in Year 12, I would sit and look at the students facing me in the assembly room each morning and ask myself how they could bear to look at my ugly face. Throughout my school days I hung back from making friends because I felt no-one would ever want to be friends with me.

And yet, they did look at me… They did seem to like me…

They did make friends with me. I did have other boyfriends after Brian and Michael. Friendship to me has always been a very special privilege to share with someone. However, I do feel that I value friendship more than those who befriend me. I think it's because I give, and others want to take. I have learned this lesson in my life that people see in me something they want. This has not prevented me developing friendships with these people, but it does arouse my awareness of what my friendship really means to them. So, I am cautious about who I befriend in my current life.

I'm a pragmatist – a realist. Knowing that most people in life want what they can get from life, including friendships, never deterred me from making friends with people I connected to. I was never negative in any way towards any friendship I developed. If someone wanted the shirt off my back, I willingly gave it. Literally – I did that once.

"Susanna, I love your shirt."

When this lady had persisted on where she could buy a similar one, I had simply taken mine off and given it to her. She had been delighted! It had been brand new and only worn for a couple of moments, so I knew it was clean!

I recently wrote this poem after a long, lost friend suddenly turned up on my doorstep wanting free coffee and cake. When I asked why she had called, she had nervously smiled and said, "Sorry, the coffee shops were closed."

I had smiled and said, "Come in, I'll make you a cappuccino."

We had then talked for hours. It made me realise there were others in my life I hadn't seen for a while, and that perhaps I should make contact.

A Time to Talk

I think I'll call my friend tonight
And ask if there's a time to talk.
I haven't seen her for a while
And hope that life is kind to her.
What is a friend, I ask myself?
If friends call me, I don't stand still,
I don't ignore a call for help
Instead, I call back loud and clear.
I might be lost in trains of thought
Or deep in hollows hoeing soil
Or working at some lab'rers toil
I'll still accept this time to chat.
When a friend drops in for coffee
And brings me a bunch of roses
My door is always open wide
With gracious smile to come inside.
If I be caught in busyness,
Would I rebuff this friend's request?
Or would I shout out to the hills
I'd love to share this time to talk.
Yes, of course I would.

This story is the final year of my schooling. I spent most of my time at school teaching English and French to the junior classes. I finished all my examinations in June of 1969 and was hoping to be accepted into college to start in September.

I had submitted my preferences through the usual channels and on June 20th 1969, I was offered an interview at Bedford Physical Education College. Obviously, my mother had opened the letter and resealed it. It was what she always did. There was never any privacy with my mail.

"Susan, I will drive you," she had said. "It will give me a chance to take out one of my patients for the day."

I could have caught the train to London, and then to Bedford, but I knew she would not have permitted me that luxury. No, I had to travel with my mother. Not only was she a terrible driver, but I had to sit in the back, as her patient needed the front seat. At the time, I knew this was more than a kind gesture to drive me, as she had always been opposed to me going to college, but I couldn't have known what her ploy was.

The interview for me went very well. The first section was a practical demonstration of gymnastic and athletic skills. My mother and her patient were the only observers in the gymnasium, but I didn't let this deter me. I performed well. I was a good gymnast and athlete, having competed in competitions at levels above school level. I was also a good games player. I played netball for my school and later in life played for North Wales. To teach Physical Education was a good career choice for me. I had initially wanted to teach French, but after speaking to the School Career Advisor I had been persuaded to change my discipline to Physical Education and Health Studies.

Watching the other participants that afternoon, I knew that my level of ability was better than most of the girls. My mother obviously recognised that her daughter stood a chance of being accepted into this college. I had chosen Bedford because it offered an all-round specialist program of study in the areas of physical education that I most enjoyed. It was also within close, proximity to London, with an opportunity to stay in college lodgings.

On entering the gates of the college that day, I had felt so proud. The beautiful sandstone buildings were close to the city centre, making it an easy commute from my house. The interior of the facilities was inspiring. I was honoured to be attending for an interview here, and I had walked in with pride.

After the practical assessment, each interviewee was required to attend a private questioning session with one of the designated staff interviewers. My interview was with the Dean of the college. She was friendly, but very particular about the answers she wanted. She grilled me intently on so many areas of my knowledge and skills across all areas of sport and health. She was impressed with my Outward-Bound experiences, as well as my school leadership roles. I was the only student at my school to be elected School Captain for two consecutive years. I felt that I had done well in this interview. I have always had a natural ability to speak in front of other people, either within the face-to-face interview setting or the public speaking forum, and so I had no reason to think that I would not be successful.

Oh, how wrong was I!

Oh, the very reason my mother was there!

Of course, she could not let me be successful. She had spent my whole childhood trying to destroy my chances of getting into college, so she certainly wasn't going to let me be successful now.

I had showered and changed into my day clothes before meeting up with my mother outside the gates of the college. She and her patient had not been permitted to wait inside the buildings during the formal interviews, and so she had taken her friend to a local tea house.

As I approached the exit gates, I saw the pair waiting anxiously outside. My mother was fidgety, unable to speak or look at me. She never spoke to me, even though I looked directly at her. She wasn't there! Her mind was not there – she was beside herself with anger - so much anger - that her mind had slipped into that realm of madness I had seen on so many occasions in my life before. It was that time when she did not know how to react but knew she had to do something.

At last, the penny dropped. I could see it in her eyes before I saw her demeanour change. She had then breathed a sigh of relief as she had decided on her plan. Looking now directly at me, she had said, "I've left my umbrella inside. I'd better go and get it."

I couldn't stop her. She had not had an umbrella that day. It had not rained – in fact it had been warm and sunny all day. I knew what she was going to do, as I watched her charge back into the building. She had then returned about ten minutes later in a calm and euphoric mood. Her eyes were glassed over. I had seen that look many times in my life before too. It was a state of euphoria in which she derived considerable gratification for doing something bad to me. To me it equated to a sexual high. She derived sexual gratification whenever she committed acts of such evil towards me. What she did to me that day was pure evil. What mother deliberately sabotages her daughter's future, especially when she has known how hard her daughter has worked to achieve this opportunity?

I have no idea what my mother's discussion had been with the Dean of the college that afternoon, all I know is that four days later I received a letter advising me of my unsuccessful interview and that my file would be passed back to the Clearing House.

I knew what this meant for me. It meant my second to fifth options would now not be considered. The only chance I had of getting into college was to hope there were still some places left at the college that offered a Physical Education Wing course.

As I lay in bed that night, I was fearful for my future as a teacher. Even if I did get offered a place at my last option, my mother would see the letter before me and sabotage this too. My only option was to contact the Clearing House and request any correspondence relating to an interview offer be sent to my school.

Which it was a month later.

My mother knew nothing about it! The college was in North Wales near Chester. It would mean having to stay overnight, something that the college organised. I spoke to my father about keeping this plan a secret. He needed to know where I would be that night. (I couldn't imagine the conversation my parents would have had about this, nor did I want to know – I just know my mother would have suspected I'd attended an interview somewhere, and that this time she could do nothing about it).

Or so I thought!

I went. I returned. I said nothing about it to my mother and she said nothing to me.

It was four days later when the principal of my school announced at the assembly that I had been successful in getting into college to train as a teacher. I was so happy. I knew that I would receive this same letter in the post at my house today, and so went home happy. There were very few times in my life up to this point that I can honestly say, I was happy. Today, though, I was. I had set my sights on becoming a teacher since I first taught my friends to ride their bikes or do gymnastics. I had overcome difficult circumstances to achieve my objective. I had a right to be happy.

As always, on entering the house that day I dropped my schoolbag in the hall and went into the kitchen to make myself some coffee. My mother was standing with her back to me, facing the boiler, as I filled the jug and prepared my coffee.

"There's a letter for you in the hall."

"I know. I saw it as I came in."

She turned around to face me. This is no word of a lie. What I saw that day I will never forget. It wasn't in my imagination. Her face was thunder. From the centre of her body poured black smoke that wafted towards me as a voice, deep from within her, spoke the words, "You'd better go upstairs!"

These words were enunciated very slowly with a deep, voice – deeper than any female or male voice I had heard spoken before. I could do nothing except stare at the blackness in front of me. I wasn't scared of the voice, or the person (if at that point in time my mother was a 'person') and I couldn't absorb the enormity of the situation. My mind simply froze in time and like a zombie I exited the room, collected my letter, and headed upstairs.

The stairs had three sets of flights that led to the upper rooms. I stopped on the first flight and opened my letter. The contents congratulated me. I was euphoric. Even though I had known all day that I had been offered a place at Cartrefle College, North Wales, to read it in print made it real. This now could not be taken away from me.

As I stepped onto the next flight, I suddenly felt an overwhelming sense of fear. What was I going to find on opening my bedroom door? On the one hand I felt such elation at getting into college, and yet on the other hand I felt such fear and dread at what I suspected my mother might have done. This juxtaposition is something I had not experienced to this level before and never would again. It was such a profoundly momentous feeling that it would remain with me for the rest of my life.

Cautiously, I stepped up the remaining stairs and opened the door.

There was nothing there. Well, there was a bed frame but no mattress or covers. There was a bare bedside table – all contents had been removed – all my French souvenirs and photographs, there was my wardrobe but no clothes inside, and there was my cupboard that still had all the food items stored, but all my schoolbooks and other schoolwork had been removed.

I had nothing left. There was not a single possession of mine in that room. How was I supposed to feel or react?

Looking out of the window, I saw an enormous pile of burning items in the middle of the lawn. The stack of debris was smouldering. My mind went into shock that afternoon. I stared at the fire from four p.m. until eight p.m. when it became dark and I was so cold, I was numb. My mind was numb. I could not fathom what my mother had done that day.

On opening my letter, and reading that I had been successful, all I can assume is that this had sent her mad, as mad as she had been the day she had hacked up my father's antique piano. In trying to understand what had occurred that day, I believe that she had been possessed. She had gone into an uncontrollable rage, grabbing every single item I owned, including my bedding, and thrown it out of the window. The mattress she must have hauled downstairs and out into the garden. Once everything was in a mound, she had set fire to all my possessions.

My question remains today, "Why did my father not do anything? He would have seen the burning mass. He would have smelt the burning fabrics. My mother would have had no excuse this time for why she had done what she had done. And yet, he did nothing!

I stood absolutely, still, frozen in time and mind. My eyes did not take their sights off the burning mass. I just stood staring until I became so cold that my mind came out of its trance-like state. As I began to return to some level of conscious state, I could feel the evil in the air in that room and I could sense the evil scent of hatred. I felt nothing for my mother – no hatred, no disgust, no sense of anger or pity – I felt totally devoid of any emotion. I was ice cold, and outside it was now too dark to see the burning embers. I left that room. I left that house, and I walked the streets until two a.m. I spoke to no-one. I have no idea where I went.

When I returned to the house, I washed my clothes and hung them in the airing cupboard to dry. I then lay in the bath for an hour, wrapped myself in a towel, slept in the bath for an hour and then got up to iron my clothes for school. I then left. I still had a couple of weeks of the school year left, and I knew I couldn't live in that house any more. My school friend, Lynne, let me stay in her room until school finished, and then I headed off to the orphanage for the summer. Lynne's mum bought me some clothes. Both she and Lynne were always so kind to me, and they never asked for anything from me. I was so grateful.

At the end of my holiday stint in Tunbridge Wells, I returned to my parent's house for the one night remaining before I trekked off to college. (A mattress and bedding had been placed on my bed – something I was pleased about, as the bath had been so uncomfortable).

My father came with me to the London mainline station that would take me to Chester. He never spoke about what had occurred. He just smiled and waved me good luck.

Sitting in that First-Class compartment that day, I felt so excited. I was off to college.

I had done it! I had gone through that tunnel and come out the other end. I was going to be a teacher and I felt so proud!

"Yay! I'm going to be a teacher!" I said quietly aloud to myself.

Live for Today

Live for today,
As you don't know what's around the corner.
Treasure what you have –
Your loved ones,
Your health,
Your beauty,
The sun and rain, wind and snow, and flowers.
Don't waste your time –
So many people just drift through their lives
Without knowing what
They really want.
They buy,
They party,
They collect all manner or useless things.
Care for others,
As you don't know when you will need their help.
Be not quick to judge
Others' faults,
Their looks,
Their habits,
But look to the purity of their souls.
If you do this
You will receive your rewards in due course,
And you will have found
Your true self,

Understanding,
Happiness,
And a genuine insight into love.

The Aftermath

If we didn't have the lows, then we wouldn't appreciate the highs! This is the juxtaposition of life – we have wet and dry seasons, cold and hot weather and daylight and darkness. Our emotions can turn from high to low or from low to high in a second, like a sudden breeze that whips up from nowhere suddenly making us shiver when its 100 degrees in the shade, or gasp with heat when snow lays on the ground in the depths of winter.

Happiness is found where one's heart is at peace, and one has unconditional love for self.

Happiness is not a state of mind I ever found at any time in my childhood. I say that with absolute and ultimate conviction, even though there were brief times I enjoyed. At the age of fifteen I knew the key to survival was having strategies to cope each day – and each day was different. On Monday mornings, walking to school, I would feel a heavy weight physically being lifted off my shoulders, and I knew I could survive the weekdays until Friday afternoon. My routine took me to the library most nights, where I would diligently complete my homework before ambling home to make coffee at an hour when I knew my parents would be in bed.

On Friday afternoons at two thirty p.m. the black weighted cloud would make its unwelcome appearance once more, bearing down on me, forcing me to walk with my head close to my knees. A teacher once passed me at this precise time and said, "Sue, you look like death!"

I was death. I couldn't survive the weekends and I was fearful of the impact on my fragile emotional state. The days I could escape, but the evenings placed great strain on my nerves. During my childhood years people didn't have music machines, I-pads, mobile phones or headphones. Headphones would have helped – I could have blocked out any external noise and retreated to the inner sanctuary of my mind. No, we had a television. Everyone watched television from six p.m. till late. The lounge room was the only warmish room in the house.

Both my parents smoked cigarettes. My father enjoyed his pipe and cigars too but did at times endeavour to give up. My mother never made any attempt to quit her habit, smoking constantly through every waking second of her day with no care or thought for how this habit affected others. The worst aspect was her morning coughing ritual. Listening to someone coughing their guts up for extensive periods of time each morning is not a pleasant thing. Why would anyone do that to themselves?

In planning my daily survival techniques, the holiday breaks were the most difficult. If I had told my mother what my plans were to be, she would have thwarted them. How I approached the news of my plans to her had to be carefully scripted at strategically delivered times.

Yes, we had rows about why, what, where, with or whom, but in the end, I always won these battles – partly, I think, because I knew there was no way I could have stayed at home for any amount of time. When you know your priority is to survive, you become very resilient to anything that will jeopardise that.

When anyone experiences significant trauma, even just one event, there is always an aftermath. Counselling services are now available to support people who suffer events that can have an emotional impact. My life from the time I was two years old, was one colossal emotional event. Never a day would pass when I didn't have to squeeze out the emotion that built up inside me. It took hours every day, and it had to be done furtively. There are times in my current life in which I still feel the need to keep squeezing.

The aftermath for me didn't start immediately. It happened gradually as doors began opening in my brain that had remained closed for many years. The first door was the one I closed after being repeatedly raped and sexually assaulted when I was six years old.

The college lifestyle was great. I loved the freedom to attend lectures, play sport and spend time with friends I made. Most of the young boys on the course played rugby for Welsh clubs and even Wales. One boy I became very good friends with was a Welsh champion boxer. Most of these lads were excellent sportsmen but relied heavily on their female conterparts to help them with their essays.

As I stayed in lodgings during term time, I always had to find residential holiday work during vacation periods, of which the first was Christmas 1969. For these four weeks I worked at a boarding school for boys that catered for their boarders, plus a holiday program of sport, craft and games activities. I was employed as the sport organiser for the course and another teacher - John – was employed to run the art and craft program. John was a lecturer in Psychology and Philosophy of Education at a university in the north of England. This boarding school was near Tunbridge Wells in the south of England, (opposite ends of the country) and so I had found it odd that John had left his wife and young family to work during this time. Christmas is a family time.

I found it even more odd that John sought my company for more than just friendship. We became accustomed to playing squash late at night, and then having drinks in my room. The first night he made his sexual advances towards me, he had said, "My goodness, Sue, you're terrified!"

He had stopped and we had talked all night. I disclosed things to him that I had buried for thirteen years. When I look back on my life, what I find interesting is that there was always someone especially chosen to help me get through the aftermath. John was such a clever counsellor and perfectly placed to hear my story. Although one becomes very upset by the opening of doors, it is the only way to begin the healing process. John was instrumental in helping me rebuild my sense of self, dignity and well-being.

The next significant holiday period was summer 1970. A friend from college and myself secured jobs as chalet maids at a Butlins Holiday Camp. I hated this job because I was so allergic to the blankets, that I suffered badly from the dust, but I was safe and away from home, so that was all that mattered.

The next door to open was the assault door. It had happened one night when my friend and I had strolled down to the village to buy our dinner and sit by the sea. On reaching a parkland area, I had heard motorbikes getting louder. Three bikes each with two occupants careered into the roadway leading to the park.

For some reason I had known I was their victim, and I had sensed that it was an initiation ceremony. There was no way these punks were going to have their way with me that night!

I have told this story in all my books for different reasons. That night one of the gang grabbed me and pulled me into their horseshoe ring that they had set up adjacent to the park. Dozens of holidaymakers were strolling around the shops and sitting on sidewalks and yet no-one came to my aid.

Once in the ring, the bikie member had begun his assault on me, but had found that I was much too skilled in self-defence tactics to allow him to proceed. I had chopped him on his clavicle nerve and punched him in the face, before re-joining my friend for our walk and dinner. None of the other bikie members had made any advances towards me after they had seen their newest recruit lying unconscious on the ground.

The significance of this incident for me was the awakening of the memories I had hidden in my brain that related to any of the physical or sexual assaults I had encountered. This assault had been a random selection, not someone who had wanted specifically to do me harm. Consequently, I never let this assault affect me in any way, unlike most people who see such an assault as so traumatic that they need extensive counselling afterwards. Not me - I just brushed my hands off and forgot about it until I was lying in bed that night.

That's when the aftermath struck. It always strikes when one is least expecting it – that moment of vulnerability. It struck me when I was not expecting it. It smacked me when I was most vulnerable. Without any prior warning, my body began to convulse and shiver violently. I couldn't stop my arms and legs from shaking out of control or my entire body from shivering. Lying in my warm bed, I became intensely cold, and I sensed a panic inside me that I couldn't control for quite some time. These memories now having surfaced, I knew would remain foremost in my mind, but which I also knew were a necessary part of the healing process. So, I let the aftermath wreak his vengeance on me until he had exhausted me, and then left me to sleep.

It's never that simple, though. He returned every day that I spent in college from that point on. On the outside I tried to appear calm and in control, but on the inside, I was anything but normal. This juxtaposition was not new to me. I had become the master of disguises and so wore the anorexia and feelings of worthlessness in secrecy. In 1971 I tried to close the door on the aftermath, but he was much too strong and just pushed it wide open.

By Christmas 1971, I had become so ill that I was hospitalised for most of that vacation period. None of my family ever visited me, and no-one else contacted me during that time. Of course, this didn't help with the healing process. I don't think I'd ever felt so utterly alone in my life. I was used to dealing with my emotional responses myself, and so I let each day come and go, knowing that time would be the best healer.

In September 1972, I commenced my teaching position at Gray's Comprehensive in Essex. These new challenges for me, as well as a new way of life socially, helped me to focus on the positives in building my life. I began dating many of my colleagues at work, as well as playing netball for the county I was living in. I lived on Canvey Island, near Southend, sharing a house with three other teachers. I enjoyed my life there and knew that professionally I would be successful as a teacher.

It amused me one day, when one boyfriend – Mick Prentice – a history teacher at my school, having met my flatmates had said, "Fuck, Susanna, you're the only sane one here!"

I had smiled. That was such a compliment. It also affirmed how successful I was at hiding my true self, and that on the outside I appeared normal, sane and in control. (I was keeping the beast at bay! I was gaining more power over him in a way that allowed me to finally close that door).

It wasn't until February 1975, that the door opened again. Again, the beast attacked me when I was most vulnerable. I had emigrated to Australia in August 1974 and begun teaching at East Hills Girls High School. At the start of the following year, I once more became sick, so sick I almost died and had to have an emergency operation.

No-one from my family made any contact with me during the time I was in hospital or afterwards. (In my current life, if my daughter had ever needed an operation, I would have instantly been at her bedside, or would be at any stage in her life!)

On returning home and resuming my usual work and home life, I fell prey to the aftermath and everything he threw at me. I became sick when eating any food, and so stopped eating until my body could take no more of that punishment. This then translated to bulimia, a condition that haunted me for over thirty years before I could finally manage my daily intake of food in a successful way.

Eating disorders are an emotional response. They are a mental health condition that, once taken hold, is incredibly hard to shake off. A smoker can quit smoking by not buying and smoking cigarettes, but the human body needs food. The slightest smell of food can entice the wrong reaction.

My problems centred around feeling worthless and unclean. Even though I was good at my job, successful in my relationships with girlfriends and boyfriends, I still had that underlying nagging that I was subordinate in some way. The feeling of being unclean came from two sources, one from my childhood at never being physically clean, and the other the internal effects of being raped so many times. Purging oneself of all internal deposits helps to make one feel clean – or at least attempts to – the feeling comes back though – too quickly. The sense of being cleansed is short-lived.

At this time in my life my weight was at its lowest it had

ever been. To try to control the bulimia my diet consisted entirely of apples. I lived on three apples a day for three years. In August of 1976, I began receiving demands from my parents to return home. My sister was getting married at Christmas time and they needed me to help with the wedding.

In the lead up to leaving, I began having nightmares. I would wake up shivering, screaming or in the throes of a panic attack. I decided to seek advice from a psychiatrist, primarily for advice about whether I should go home, but also to seek some treatment for the emotional disorders I was experiencing.

In November 1976 I sat in the psychiatrist's chair wearing casual cotton clothes, and in the two-hour session I disclosed my entire life story. On leaving his rooms and entering the street, I suddenly became aware that my clothes were as saturated with sweat as if I'd just stepped out of a swimming pool of water fully clothed. I was soaking wet, but I hadn't realised the moisture from my body had been building up at any time during the consultation. (He must have noticed it though – but he didn't say anything!)

Even my hair was soaking wet! I hadn't noticed the drips from my hair or clothes until I stepped into the street. The advice I was given from this doctor that day, was to never make any contact again with my mother. Good advice, sound advice – but I knew I couldn't follow it. I knew I had to go!

And so, I did.

"Come on, get up!"

It is six a.m. on the first morning after I had arrived back in Harrow. I was staying at my older sister, Justine's house, as there was no way I could consider staying at my parent's house. Justine's house was only a short walk away from our family house. I know that my parents had been furious at my decision to stay with Justine, and I was fully aware of the aggressive arguments that had ensued, but that was their problem – not mine. I felt I was entitled to choose to stay with Justine.

I had arrived at her house around eleven thirty p.m. and suffering from jetlag, I had been glad to sleep for a few hours. A few hours, though, was all I was allowed! My mother had barged into the room where I was sleeping, pulled back the curtains and ordered me to get up.

Justine and her husband were still asleep in their room and had not been aware our mother had entered the house.

"How come she has a key?" I had asked my sister later that day.

"Yes, that was a mistake," Justine had replied.

"Well, you need to get it back off her!" I had looked sternly at my sister.

"That won't be easy – she had insisted she have one."

And so, I got up. I spent the whole day cooking for Christine's wedding the next day. No-one said any word of thank you, even after I had cleaned the house later that night. About to leave to return to Justine's house, my mother had said, "You'll be here by ten thirty in the morning ready for the church."

"No-one has given me an invitation," I had just looked at my mother.

She had then got up, scrawled me a scrappy note on a piece of scrap paper and handed it to me. "Now you're invited."

And so, I went. I played the dutiful host all day, serving food and drinks to guests who wondered who I was. I had just smiled at them. Having lived away from home for seven years, I had disconnected from my family, something I felt no regret for. None of these people who professed to being friends of my family, showed any interest in me during the times I was critically ill, and so I felt no interest in getting to know any of them. I was simply the unpaid hired help of the day.

Returning to Sydney afterwards, I felt a huge weight lifted off my shoulders. My parents had thought I had returned home for good. They had been surprised when they had seen me packing, and said, "Are you leaving?"

I had looked blankly at the pair of them and said, "I'm going home."

I recalled an argument I had once had with my mother when I was thirteen years old and smiled to myself. She had slapped me hard across the face and yelled at me, "You'll never leave home!"

"Yes, I will. I want to do Voluntary Service Overseas for two years. I don't care where I go." I had shown her no emotion.

She had laughed and said, "No-one is going to accept you into that program."

I think my mother was so intensely annoyed at my success in life. She had tried so hard to stop me from training as a teacher, and equally devilishly to thwart my boyfriend plans and now I sensed her intent to block my return to Sydney. No way! No way would she now stop me from leaving. I knew I no longer belonged in Harrow with my family. My home was in Australia where my flat was, my job was and where my husband to be, was.

In thinking about how I came to choose Australia, it had been because of my friend Sandy.

It had been during our college years that we had met. Sandy's mother had died of breast cancer when Sandy had been thirteen years old. She had lived in Sydney, near Coogee Beach. I remained friends with Sandy after we both began working as teachers. In 1974, the Australian Government offered opportunities for English teachers to work in Australian schools, and Sandy and I applied to work in Sydney. We had initially intended only to do the two years on offer, but having settled in our schools, we decided to stay. The American teachers, who had also been recruited, were only permitted to work in Australia for two years. Sandy and I had no such limitations.

We both loved our lifestyles in Sydney, and we remained firm friends until the cancer gene struck Sandy too a few years later.

1977 saw me establish myself in my school and begin to build my career. I enjoyed my teaching schedules as well as the freedom to live my life as I wished. The aftermath, however, accompanied me wherever I went.

To address my emotional issues, I sought the assistance of a trauma hypnotherapist. He specialised in working with people who had been raped. I attended two sessions before I couldn't take any more. After each session, I would have horrible nightmares, followed by obsessive thoughts of hatred towards my mother that set me into a deep depressive state. The hypnosis had opened doors that had been long closed, and which I did not want to open.

The hypnotherapy technique took away any emotion I felt to anything in life. Even to this day, I find it really, hard to be emotional about anything. If I am given gifts, people are surprised I seem thankless. I'm not, really – I just cannot show gratitude. Likewise, I cannot cry. I cannot let the tears fall, much as I want to sometimes.

Following my husband's death after a cancerous brain tumour, I had wanted to grieve by crying it out of my system, but no matter how hard I tried, the tears would only fall on the inside, not the outside.

So, this was my life and I accepted it. I accepted that the

aftermath would be with me for many years, and I had to gradually work at him to release his hold on me. Thirty-five years later, I was finally able to say I had got my bulimia under control. Fuck – that was way too long!

My thanks go to my lovely husband who supported me unconditionally throughout our lives together.

A Soft Touch

A soft touch at close of day,
A gentle shiver down my spine,
These subtle signs just let me know
That you're still there.
A quiet voice in my head
When decisions I have to make,
You always give me good advice –
For you're still there.
Among the busy hours of day,
In push and shove I lose my way.
I know you're with me all the time –
That you still care.
When we shared life together,
We took for granted special times,
And I never thought I'd lose you –
For you were there.
We still live life together.
I feel you with me everywhere.
I shouldn't mourn and grieve so,
Because you're there.

The Epilogue

In looking back at my childhood through this memoir, I have lain my life bare for all to view. I have been honest but not overly descriptive in times of extreme privacy, such as in providing the details of the cunnilingus and fellatio acts I either had to endure or be subjected to perform on the gentlemen my mother had selected for her amusement and no doubt – enjoyment.

During the Sunday afternoons in that scullery kitchen adjacent to my home kitchen, I could smell my mother's cigarette smoke wafting through the wall, and I could feel her presence nearby. I would be required to lie on a board, over a bath, which was positioned against the connecting wall.

I would hear the glass being positioned against this wall and knew that she was listening.

What mother does that to her child?

I have two children, now both adults, and it is still my job to love them, as I do unconditionally. I write my stories, poems and blogs for an adult audience, and in so doing use a language code to imply the level of anger or inappropriateness I feel towards any situation I have been forced to endure.

A modicum of inappropriateness finds me using the word 'fuck.' It was an unacceptable act or situation warranting an unacceptable descriptive word.

A serious level of inappropriateness requires a far more serious tone inferred on this word. It is fucking, unacceptable that any child of five years old, or at any age of childhood or at any age of adulthood, be exposed to such sexual acts of deviancy. For a mother to orchestrate the acts, condone them and then enjoy responding to them, is beyond fucking – there are no words to describe this depravity.

I make no apologies for this language code as I make no apologies to any reader who takes umbrage by these recounts. There are some stories that must be told.

At no time in my childhood did I ever refer to my mother as 'mummy' or 'mum' or 'mama' or any similar word of endearment towards the person who bore me. It is the first word a child says as he/she begins to speak. Why was this word so vile to my mother, that she could not be called it? I cannot answer this question because the truth lies in the experiences she was subjected to in her childhood.

At no time in my childhood did my mother ever say a kind word to me, blow me a soft kiss or gently pat or stroke my hair. I see parents caressing their children like this every day when I am teaching them. The only words ever spoken to me were castigatory ones. Was she so unhappy as a mother or as a wife or as an adult person that she could only think negatively towards her child? I could have understood why this was, if I had antagonised her in some way, but I learned early on in my life that I had to be good – beyond good. If she was so cruel to me when I was so good, what would she have done to me if I had done something wrong?

Throughout my entire childhood she expected me to be her subservient slave. I never saw her lift a finger to clean the house, or the silver, or the brassware or the toilets, or the steps outside the house that for some bizarre reason had to be cleaned when snow lay like a carpet over them. No, those duties were reserved for me. How does a baby at two years of age wash nappies for a six-week-old baby? How does that same child six months later do the family washing using a tub, a mangle and a clothing hoist?

Can anyone out there tell me how a mother can deliberately make her child sick and leave her to die, and why no-one saw it necessary to ever (I'm going to repeat that) ever, take any action against her?

A friend of mine, the lady this book is dedicated to, provided me with some rationale and I'd like to include this here.

'These are so very shocking... these incidents, as well you would know, all fall under the umbrella of child abuse (physical abuse, sexual abuse & exploitation, emotional abuse, neglect, subjugation & domestic slavery). Every box is being ticked. Whether or not she learned this awful behaviour herself as a child, or whether or not she was sexually abused herself as a child, there's just no excuse for such a perversion of trust.

At first, I decided your mother was a cruel sexual deviant who got pleasure from your suffering, but whilst reading it this time around, it strikes me that your family operated a bit like a cult, with your mother being the self- appointed, all controlling, punishing, never to be questioned, leader. All the members of the family (cult) were powerless, their voices suppressed, presumably because they were afraid of the consequences of disobedience. Yet she maintained a veneer of normalcy for others to see - for example she went to work & held down a respectable job and had friends over for tea (yes, I know that psychopaths can pass off as 'normal' if they want to). You and your sisters had no power because you were kids! With no money, nowhere to go, no voice, not to mention absent/undeveloped/distorted critical thinking skills.

I do wonder (what the fuck) your father was thinking. He must have known - if not about the sexual abuse of you then, surely, he was aware of the cruelty. Did you ever broach it with him in later years? Was he afraid of your mother too or just the stigma of divorce? I imagine that in those days in the UK, divorce was handled similarly to Australia pre-1975, where it was a matter of proving blame on the other party, such as drunkenness, abandonment, cruelty or the like. I know you can't always get answers, satisfactorily or otherwise.

Rosemary, I never discussed any issue with my father because from an early age I knew innately that it was part of my life plan to be subjected to this life – for whatever lessons I needed to learn (I will come back to this idea later in this section). I knew that my father was also subjected to her vicious assaults on his person, possessions and good nature. She knew he was a weak man.

At the end of the war, he had fallen in love with this gorgeous looking lady who had been his nurse. She had targeted him from the onset. Once home in England, my father had immediately realised his mistake. He had known his wife's mother was mad. She had been placed in a mental institution. Neither of my parents ever visited and my mother never spoke of her. No-one even mentioned when she passed, and neither of them attended her funeral.

When my mother began showing bizarre behaviours towards him, I think he was so fearful of the consequences that he went into denial and chose to ignore all events. He survived his early married years by returning home late each night and isolating himself in his room listening to music.

During one of my psychic sessions with a medium, my father spoke to me. There were many times he spoke to me in similar sessions:

Mary (psychic friend of mine): Sue your father just smiled

and said, "You know Mary, today Susie put out a photo of us on her wedding day."

Mary: Did you?

Me: I didn't, no, but my husband did. Michael had placed a photo of my father and myself walking down the church aisle on our dresser that very morning. Mike and I had then had a conversation about him. He must have been watching and listening.

Mary: Yes, Sue, he was.

In a more recent session, this conversation occurred:

Mary: Sue, your father wants to talk to you.

Me: I can feel him in the room.

Mary: He says he is so sorry for the things that happened to you. He says he was a weak man, who was selfish. He only thought of his own needs during those awful times. He says he knew what went on but did not know what to do about any of them.

In my current life I am fascinated by the opportunities that exist to travel into the realm of 'Life Between Lives.' I have undergone this type of regression now three times. The last journey I made took me into the cell where I worked as a researcher, researching mental health strategies. As I came into the stone building that day, I immediately noticed my husband seemingly in charge of the activities that were occurring. Everyone in the area was very busy handing him information, exchanging information or burying their bodies in reading matter to look up information to give to him. It was then Michael's job to cross the floor – he was the only soul permitted to cross from our cell to the entrances where the messengers would deliver their information to him.

Watching these proceedings for me was interesting because

Michael was never a leader in his physical life, but in this realm, he was clearly the one in charge.

I had then seen my father. He was sitting lying back in a large chair watching me with no expression on his face except a deep sense of sadness. His frame was much bigger than in his physical life, almost overweight, which was something he never was anytime I knew him during his life.

Thinking about this moment, I think he was projecting to me his deep and profound understanding of how sad he was that he had not helped me when I had needed him to. So, yes, Rosemary, you can get answers!

This quote from L.P. Hartley* in his novel, 'The Go-Between' (1953) * L.P. Hartley – British novelist, 1895 – 1972.

'The past is a foreign country: they do things differently there,' is very apt as is this one, 'How we understand the past and how we come to terms with our own memories, is an unpaid debt that all humans share.' (Andrés L. Córdova in The Hill)

I have come to terms with my memories through my spiritual awakening. In all the books that I have written I have described situations in which I have been in the presence of 'spirit.'

1965: My spirit guide (Ahman) came to me one night to prevent me from committing suicide and to guide me towards the belief that I could be a teacher. I know that I came into this life specifically to be a teacher – nothing else – I will be teaching children on my deathbed!

1985: Ahman appeared at my car window to push my car back into the side road, just as a truck from Picton whizzed past me on its way to Campbelltown. I had been driving a manual car, when I hadn't realised I had to stop and look to my right. After Ahman's hand had pushed me to safety, I had looked at my manual car: handbrake off, gears in second, my two feet firmly on the ground, my hands on the steering wheel, car not shaking – engine purring beautifully – how can that be? I can still see his huge face on my car windscreen.

1988: A student I had been teaching collapsed and needed heart and lung resuscitation. This procedure I performed on this child many times in the time I knew her, to keep her alive. The week prior to her death, after a resuscitation episode, she had written me a letter. During the resuscitation, I had felt that this little girl had left to speak to her spirit guides. When she returned, she was different, and I knew she had made up her mind to leave.

She had cardiomyopathy and was much too small and frail for a heart transplant. In her letter, she had explained to me her reasons for leaving. I read this at her eulogy a week
   later.

After passing, she had come to me that weekend, first on the Saturday night and then the Sunday morning. On the Sunday she had been in my head from four a.m. to seven a.m. forcing me to get up and visit her mother. She needed me to channel for her. Arriving at the house the door had opened as if by magic. I had been shown inside, as if I had been expected.

The room was ready for us. This little girl then told her mother her story. It took two hours and then I left. I have no idea what I said, or rather what she said, except that afterwards I went into shock.

A few years later, I had another experience after someone had passed. It was the day of my mother-in-law's funeral, and I had gone to bed that night. All day I had felt waves of electricity going through my veins in both arms and legs. I had awoken at 12.47 a.m. dying of thirst. I never drink water but had to get up and fetch a glass from the kitchen downstairs. On the third stair, I had felt myself go giddy for just a second.

I had collected my water from the fridge and noticed the electric oven clock read 1.48 a.m. I thought there must have been a power cut upstairs. The battery clock in the kitchen also read 1.48 a.m. Thinking no more about the time, I returned to my room. Looking at my bedside clock that now read 1.48 a.m. I had dropped my water. I had lost an hour of time. Looking back, I know that I had met with my mother-in-law that night. She had been with me all day and left as soon as she had spoken to me. In our conversation she had wanted to know if I would look after her son - my husband - in his illness at the end of his life. I had assured her that I would. Michael had never wanted to go into a care centre or hospice. He had always wanted to remain at home, no matter how difficult it became for both of us. I respected his and his mother's wishes.

As well as having many other psychic experiences, I have undergone Past Life Regression on three occasions, each for different reasons, and three Life Between Lives for different reasons. When you go back into your 'other' self you become more in tune with your soul energy in which there is RNA. This RNA is the equivalent to our physical body's DNA and forms part of our Soul Structure Code. Coops, M (2021)* gives the information as, 'a complex system that is composed of seven components, each part having seven sub-components to program in preparation for life on Earth.

* Margaret Rogers Van Coops, Doctor of Philosophy & Clinical Hypnosis & Behavioural Sciences, Doctor of Integrated Medicine, USA.

Your choice is yours alone, but with the help of your Master Teacher/Spirit Guides who no longer come into embodiment, you first discuss this coding with them in preparation for another life to be lived in our future.'

In my last Life Between Lives, I met with the Council of Elders. This was my ultimate purpose for undertaking this experience, as I needed to have a conversation with them about issues unresolved from previous lives.

There was no avenue for me to do this in my current physical life. This Council is a group of souls who discuss with each incoming soul the previous life they have led and the lessons that have been learned or not learned.

The Council that day had castigated me for not living up to my expectations in my previous life and had warned that this life for me had to be a significant one. I had been given a strong message to do better!

Following this meeting, I was shown the screen where I was to choose my next life – my current life. In this auditorium were many screens and many souls discussing their next embodiments with their guides. These guides are not our spirit guides but are our new life facilitators. Here is the conversation I had with my facilitator in that moment.

"Shalana, most people have some choice about their next life. They are usually offered two choices. These choices are selected to match the lessons you must learn in your next life. These lessons are carefully prepared for you by your Master Teacher."

"My screen is blank."

I look around the room and every other soul has visual images on their screens, and they are talking animatedly with their facilitators.

"Why is my screen blank?"

"Shalana, if I show you what you are going to experience, you will not embody."

I understood that in returning to Earth for my current

lifetime, I had difficult lessons I had to learn. One of these lessons was to survive a life on Earth without committing suicide. In one of my Past Life Regressions, my spirit guides had shown me six lives, 3 in which I had committed suicide and 3 in which I had made the conscious decision not to end my life that way. One of the suicide choices was the drowning of a young man of twenty-four years of age. I clearly remember standing on a bridge looking down at muddy water swirling below me. I was tallish, wearing a brown, pin-striped suit and crisp white shirt. I had slipped into the water and felt myself go under as my lungs filled up with water. I can still feel this drowning sensation today. To aid in the drowning, I had tied a heavy stone around my left ankle, so that I could not surface once I had begun drowning – I just had to let go.

Undergoing these types of out of body experiences has helped me to look at life from another perspective. We can end our life on Earth at any time, but we can never end our life! Exiting this life for any reason, does not exonerate us from learning the lessons we must learn – they are transferred into the next life until learned.

I accept that coming into this life, I had to learn hard lessons from previous lives. When we have a significant life, we choose people on Earth who will help us achieve our life goals. Hard as this may seem, my mother was probably especially chosen by me to be that person. When we select the people in our current lives, who have been placed to help us learn our lessons, we do not choose people we do not know, we choose people who know us best. Each time we return to Earth we meet up with souls we know from past lives. We marry and have children with the same souls over and over again, but in different ways. I know that my husband has been my husband in three past lives and will be again in another life.

One of my most wonderful spiritual experiences happened before my husband passed. In a Past Life Experience, I was taken to the portal where Michael came to meet me. He had been so happy to see me, beaming and talking vividly about how wonderful life was there. He had called me by my 'pet' name – Mike and I had 'pet' names for each other that no-one else knew.

People ask me all the time how we can still be on Earth and yet in Heaven at the same time. Yes, we can. This is because we allocate a portion of our energy into each current life and leave a portion still in the spirit realm. The portion we leave in Heaven is our Higher Self. A portion of our energy always remains there – we are always connected to our Home and our Higher Self.

Seeing Michael so happy back Home, gave me great comfort in knowing that when it was his time to pass, he would still be alive, just in another form and place.

When I returned from the United Kingdom, following my last regression, I wrote this poem. I like writing poems – they help people understand complex problems written in poetic ways. This poem is published in The Lighter Side (2021) by Austin Macauley (London, UK).

Privileged Lives

We are guests in this world:
Souls creating experiences in human bodies.
We aim to bring consciousness into a material form
To create a deeper awareness of the purposes of each visit.
By understanding this,
We learn the coveted secrets of our earthly bodies
And the journeys our souls make, as we fulfil our purposes
Within the grandiose Action Plan, carefully scripted for each lifetime.
Death is just a passing,
When our souls release their hold on our physical bodies
And escape into an amazing aura of love and light,
Returning Home each time in the sanctuary of peace to review achievement.
Our lives would hold no good,
If the experience was an exclusive barony.
Understanding that perfection is reached through imperfection
Belies the wisdom that imperfection is the ultimate life-long goal.
So, we are guests in this world,
Fully accountable for every thought, deed and promise.
The more profound our metamorphosis, the deeper we love
And appreciate the ultimate privilege of spending time on Earth.

Have I ever had any communication with my mother since her passing?

Yes. I have never contacted her directly, but she has made an appearance in several psychic sessions I have engaged in. She has never spoken to me directly, nor has she said anything to the medium to be relayed to me. The most significant occasion was when the facilitator (medium – different one to Mary) had suddenly looked at me.

"Your mother is standing behind you."

"Yes, I can sense her."

"Her spirit is very light, and she is happy and bright," the medium stared at the space immediately behind my right ear.

I then felt my mother's hands around my neck, and my necklace fell off into my lap. This necklace has a clasp that is difficult to open. My mother hadn't wanted to speak to me that day, but she had wanted to let me know that she was there.

Every time I do a psychic session, no matter who the facilitator is, my parents are present. This tells me that they are always with me. They are both with me in writing this book. When I wrote my first book about my life, I was so scared to divulge any content in relation to aspects of my life, that I felt guilty for years afterwards. I was also worried that there would be some recourse for me, or that people would treat me differently. (Tears on the Inside 2011).

In writing this book, I can sense my mother's presence. Does she feel aggression or animosity towards me for telling this story? No, she does not. She understands that I had to learn lessons from her, and that she played her part. I am now recounting this impact, but in so doing am not blaming her. I have come to terms with my experiences. I never blamed her at any time throughout my childhood. I always understood that she had a mental health disorder fuelled by an intense jealousy.

I saw four personalities in my mother:

1. A happy district nurse working with her patients.

2. A very unhappy wife and mother, who felt trapped in a cocoon that she could not escape from. Her marriage had not been what she had expected, and she had never wanted children. She bore children because it was what she believed society expected of her.

3. A persona in which her deviancy resulted from unknown events from her past or genetic code, but which coerced her to commit acts of atrocities for sexual pleasure.

4. A body possessed by an evil so vile, black smoke emanated from her body for a brief moment, and through which a voice, so deep, spoke to me on one occasion.

Would I be the person I am today, if I had not experienced these events in my past? No. I have become a very mentally strong person, able to withstand any hardship or challenge thrown at me. In any subsequent life, I will never experience rape or sexual assault again. I will never have the same need again to be a teacher. I will probably have an easier life next, and hopefully one that allows me to earn money for pleasure – something this life has denied me.

I have become very psychically aware. I can read people as if I am reading a book. In meeting someone for the first time, I can glean information about them, their past experiences and future aspirations in just a few seconds. (I only disclose this information to them, though, if they specifically ask me to).

I have come to understand that our spirit guides play a large part in steering our lives. They are present with us and know our needs and lessons to learn. There is no such thing as a coincidence – our spirit guides orchestrate events for a purpose.

I recently decided to trek out to a friend's house after work to deliver her a gift of meat and fish. The meat item was a large fillet of beef that could not be purchased in a shop. I was supposed to have chosen the weekend after the one I selected, but for some reason felt impelled to go when I did.

On handing over the food items, my friend had said, "Susanna, these are perfect for our dinner party this weekend. We are having a table load of guests over."

Had I gone the week after, my friend would not have been at home, and so there would not have been any dinner party. My guides knew the exact day to pick. (I wonder if my friend had realised this. Probably not!)

My guides steer me every step of my way through my life. I can talk to Ahman and my other guide whenever I want. If I have difficult decisions to make, I talk to them at night, and when I wake in the morning – the solutions are always there. They never let me down. In encouraging other people to understand the spirit realm, I am frequently asked this question:

"Susanna, if there is a God, how come so many children live in poverty, how come so many bad things happen to people and why doesn't God do something to help them? A loving God would not let these people suffer so!"

What people do not realise is that it is not God's position to fix up the mistakes of man. If God solved our problems, we would then just expect him to, and this would not help us learn the lessons we need to learn except this message: God cleans up our messes.

He doesn't! If we create a problem – we must fix it!

In 1999 I decided to change my name. Initially this was for business purposes, but then later for enjoyment purposes. When I learned my spiritual name of Shalana, I combined this with my nickname of Sue to form the name of Susanna.

I hated being called Susan, not so much because of the name itself – I know dozens of Susans who are happy with their name – but because of the way or the tone of how it was said to me.

I love the name Susanna. I do not shorten it. I love that people call me Susanna. It is music to my ears.

I now close the door on this significant chapter of my life and only look to my future.

Truly, I can say, "I look back without anger!"

Toil and Strife

We are all brought together
By our toil and strife,
And we feel such empathy
For a troubled life.
We don't have the same bonding
When good times we share,
But we reach out more readily
To show that we care,
When our hearts become lonely
Or our grieving tears run.
Then, we search our emotions
And our souls become one.

The next two poems are for my husband, for he is always with me.

A Fleeting Embrace

A stray leaf
Brushes your shoulder
In the breeze
And sees the real you.
It sees hats
Changed like underwear
Just briefly
For the games we shared.
Your mask masks
Your soul that knows you –
The real you
Hidden deep in heart.
Your purpose
Is what defined you
Belying
What was your essence.
Through soft air
I flit and flutter
In your wake -
A fleeting embrace
A brief touch
Your quick glance sideways

Senses me
So, I stay a while
Why do I
Remain in your shadow
Like a nymph
Drifting in space.
I should leave
I've touched you gently
But I can't -
I can only wait.

A Reflect at Midnight

You graced my life for a brief, moment,
like a dew drop landing on a leaf,
before sliding off into oblivion.
Your residue,
that soft fragment of connection,
remained like a sinew-thin moon outline,
etched across a darkening sky,
until morning's light took you away.
With the passing of time
comes the dawning of sadness
that persists in the memory of time shared,
but now too is lost in life's annals,
never to flow my way again.
Life's currents spark brief interludes of hope,
but which fade too, too quickly,
into the stream of ether
as thought's molecules absorb all traces,
leaving nothing.

References

Córdova, A (2020). Thinking through history: The past is a foreign country. *The Hill*, p.2/13, accessed on 10th August 2022. <https://thehill.com>opinion>civil-rights>

Hartley, L.P. (2004) The Go-Between. *Penguin Books Australia*, accessed on 10th August 2022. <https://www.penguin.com.au>

Rogers Van Coops, M (2021). The Soul Structure Coding, Dna, Rna & The Brain. *Journal of Clinical Epidemiology and Toxicology*, p1/4, accessed on 11th August 2022. <https://www.researchgate.net>publication>35596143>

Books by Susanna Elliott-Newth

Tears on the Inside (2011) Palmer Higgs (No longer available)

The Lighter Side (2021) Austin Macauley, London, UK

Coffee Time: Come in for a Coffee and a Chat (2022) Austin Macauley, London, UK

Rags and Riches (in publication process 2023) Austin Macauley, London, UK